THE ART OF SEA TROUT FISHING

THE ART OF SEA TROUT FISHING

·Charles McLaren·

A New and Revised Edition
Edited by T. Graeme Longmuir

UNWIN

HYMAN

LONDON SYDNEY WELLINGTON

First published in Great Britain by Oliver and Boyd Ltd, 1963.
Revised edition first published in Great Britain by the Trade Division of
Unwin Hyman Limited, 1989.

Unwin Hyman Limited, 15–17 Broadwick Street, London W1V 1FP

Allen & Unwin Australia Pty Ltd
8 Napier Street, North Sydney, NSW 2060, Australia

Allen & Unwin New Zealand Pty Ltd with the Port Nicholson Press
Compusales Building, 75 Ghuznee Street,
Wellington, New Zealand

British Library Cataloguing in Publication Data
McLaren, Charles C.
The art of sea trout fishing.
1. Great Britain. Rivers. Sea trout. Angling,—Manuals
I. Title   II. Longmuir, T. Graeme
799.'755
ISBN 0-04-440406-9

Set in Times and Palatino by Cambridge Photosetting Services
and printed in Great Britain at the University Press, Cambridge

— CONTENTS —

Editor's Note

EVERY fisherman who has caught a fish owes a great deal to those who initiated him. My debt to Charles McLaren is immeasurable.

It was because I first caught a *real* fish with Charles looking over my shoulder and whispering in my ear that I eventually made my home on North Uist, one of many islands in the Outer Hebrides beloved of sea trout fishermen. It meant that I could no longer fish Loch Hope regularly from Altnaharra under Charles' watchful eye, but the friendship with Charles and his second wife, Lily, was cemented outside the fishing season.

Sadly, Charles died suddenly on his way home from the Algarve in Spring 1987, where he had begun this revision of the 1963 edition of *The Art of Sea Trout Fishing*. The friendship with Lily continued over and beyond my conduct of his funeral service in Perth.

Thus it was that Lily entrusted me with his hand-written notes and jottings, some on cardboard, others written between the lines of the first edition, along with a typescript in the hope that it might be re-published one day. Roy Eaton's further encouragement spurred me on to produce this final work from one whose words should never be forgotten by those who fish for sea trout in Scotland, and who stands as a giant amongst fishermen – albeit a gentle giant as well as a gentleman.

Both Lily McLaren and I have been greatly assisted in getting this revised edition into print, for which special thanks are due to Stephen Drummond-Sedgwick, Andy Walker, Conrad Voss Bark and Ian Hynd.

There is much I would have liked to discuss further with Charles which would have made this book as perfect as was his fishing technique – suffice it to say that Charles would have wished the final words to have been:

'The most noble of fish – the Sea Trout.'

GRAEME LONGMUIR
North Uist

Preface to the 1963 Edition

Of the three main game fish – trout, salmon and sea trout – the sea trout is the least consistently fished for, and very possibly the least understood. It is a migratory fish of great sporting value, running from early spring to late autumn into a great variety of fresh water, from humble little burns to rivers and lochs of great size. Today, more and more game fishers are setting aside periods of their season for the exclusive pursuit of sea trout since the sport given by this beautiful and powerful fish is rewarding in a way that neither salmon nor trout fishing can ever be.

Those who are unfortunate enough to fish only for sea trout in spate conditions, when the fish taken are likely to be very fresh, know only one side of the sea trout's nature. The very fresh sea trout is a free-rising fish without the crafty dourness of fresh water to make his capture difficult. Of course, a fresh fish is very powerful and very sporting, and a trophy to be justly proud of, but the deeper skills of sea trout fishing extend to the taking of fish which have taken up lies in rivers and lochs, and there without knowledge of the species, an angler might find those sea trout very difficult fish indeed.

Sea trout fishing in lochs, rivers and estuaries demands a knowledge of depths and lies and the skilled use of techniques and carefully selected tackle if the angler is to be successful. In the chapters which follow I have tried to distil what I know of sea trout in lochs and rivers in such a way that not only the techniques that I have found to be useful but also the thrill that fishing has brought me may perhaps be experienced by others.

I have been fortunate enough to spend my life in areas where sea trout run in large numbers and many of the waters I know are distinguished by fish of great size. Writing this book has given me the pleasure of reliving some of the experiences of my angling days and nights. Experience forms the background of all I want to bring to the reader's attention, and if I can communicate in this book something of the feelings of a passionate sea trout fisher as well as some of the main techniques I will be satisfied.

CHARLES C. McLAREN
Altnaharra
August 1963

Preface to the 1987 Edition

The sea trout has fallen on bad times since I wrote the 1963 edition. Disease has taken its toll – as have excessive netting at sea and in the estuaries, pollution, and the effects of drainage and afforestation with the loss of spawning areas and ample feeding.

The sea trout does not have the commercial value of the salmon and little effort has been made to protect the redds or restock the waters; indeed, some fishery owners have introduced salmon to sea trout rivers in an attempt to increase their value. This may not succeed. Nature makes the decision and sea trout waters are for sea trout.

There are, however, clear signs that the sea trout stock is building up again well, albeit better along some coasts than others, and we can help this along in a very important way by not killing finnock, the immature sea trout. The halcyon days of sea trout fishing will return, though perhaps not as of old.

Charles C. McLaren
Altnaharra
1987

FOREWORD

THE curious thing about fishing in Scotland is that most of the best books about it have been written by the English. In our own time we've had John Ashley-Cooper, Arthur Oglesby, Hugh Falkus and others, and fine books they've made of it, but unless I am much mistaken there has not been an authentic book about Highland fishing by a Highland fisherman as long as memory survives. True, we had Scrope and Stewart, but they were essentially Tweed and the Borders, though Hamish Stewart did include the Hebrides. Go north beyond the Highland Line, beyond the Grampians to the rugged hills and the lochs of Ross and Cromarty and the bleak uplands of Sutherland, and we have not had a fisherman from there to talk to us in generations.

Fortunately for us the gap was filled twenty-odd years ago by a great Highland fisherman, Charles McLaren, probably one of the greatest sea trout fishermen Scotland has known. In the first edition of *The Art of Sea Trout Fishing*, published in Edinburgh, he put down all he had learned in forty-three years of fishing the rivers and lochs that were his joy – Stack, Maree, Hope, Kinlochewe, Inver, Kirkaig, Naver, Mudale and many others. It was a remarkable book, full of surprises, telling us how to catch sea trout during the day when most of us thought the fish were impossible to take except at night, and how and why to use flies that were only about a quarter the size of the huge sunk lures that were supposed to be obligatory, and this, and that, and so much more. I remember my astonishment at reading it and the changes it wrought in my attitude of mind and my beliefs. Now, here is a better and a revised edition, edited by his friend Graeme Longmuir, for a permanent place in our libraries.

Charles McLaren was a small man in stature but a big man in his wisdom and outlook on the world. He was born in 1914 and for most of his life – apart from a short spell in the army from which he retired with a disability pension – he was a professional fisherman, a fishing instructor, and the owner or manager of some of the finest fishing hotels in Scotland. His father had the Kinlochewe Hotel and Charles was on the river there with a rod from the age of six. Later he became a manager of hotels himself, first at the Old Lodge at Lochinver, then at the Culag, and from there he bought the Altnaharra Hotel in Sutherland, where he managed the hotel himself, taught fishing, looked after the guests, and also found time to win fly-casting tournaments at Scarborough. His 64-yard salmon distance cast in 1957 remains, so far as I know, a record to this day.

There is a lovely story about him which will give you a flavour of the man. One of his guests was complaining about there being no fish in the river. Charles nodded and listened and later went out with his rod and came back with a sea trout of eight or ten pounds or so. He put it on the hall table, went to find the man who was then having dinner and said kindly and pleasantly in his ear, 'I've left a fish for you outside', and went away chuckling to himself. He was a great man. He died in 1987.

CONRAD VOSS BARK
Lifton, Devon

——1——

THE SEA TROUT

THE female sea trout deposit their ova in October and November (and occasionally later, as in the Outer Hebrides) in gravel in a stream of fresh water, where they are fertilised by the males, and that is the end of parental interest in the welfare of the eggs. It is indeed all the parental interest needed, because great care has been taken in the selection of the gravel bed. A reasonable depth is needed, so that the female may make the redd and the water can run down and back through the stones, as well as over them. When the eggs are laid they are carried down amongst the stones with the milt released by the male.

The eggs remain there during the incubation period, which is about three months, depending on the temperature of the water. High temperature reduces the incubation period and low temperature lengthens it. The eggs are usually assured of sufficient moisture for survival. They can endure being frozen, but redds and eggs may be damaged at the thaw, when ice-floes break up and bruise the eggs or expose them to fish or fowl, always eager to enjoy such a succulent bite as sea trout ova. Each female lays a great many eggs, about seven or eight hundred for each pound of her weight. But only a very small percentage of them reach the small sea trout stage, and it is not fully known how many of these eventually return to spawn.

Alevins

THE eggs hatch out into alevins – small fish with yolk-sacs dangling beneath their bellies. The yolk-sac provides nourishment until the tiny fish is able to fend for itself and, now called a fry, begins to venture comparatively far afield. One of the greatest of all the enemies of the alevin is the voracious dragonfly larva. No doubt many people have seen dragonflies lay their eggs on the water and admired them, little thinking of the tremendous damage the larvae do to fish.

Parr and Smolts

AFTER a few weeks the fry become sea trout parr, which do not have such readily seen fingermarks on their flanks as salmon parr. The length of their stay in freshwater as parr varies from two to four years, on average three. Then in May or later they don a silvery coat and move downstream as smolts to the coastal waters of the estuary where, in general, they feed well and grow rapidly without appearing to go far from the coast.

Finnock

THE smolts grow and become finnock* and return to their native water during the summer. Some of these finnock spawn and some feed on the spilled ova of spawning sea trout and salmon. Finnock return to the sea at various times. Some seem to return almost immediately while others stay in rivers and freshwater lochs until the following April.

The adult sea trout return to the rivers at any time from June to October, though a few do come back in April. Then, in the back end and during spates, they ascend small streams and spawn there, or they may spawn in the main river. I have seen thousands of sea trout spawning in small streams, some huge fish in ditches roofed over with rushes beside the road, their presence betrayed only by the sound of their splashing.

Kelts

WHEN the sea trout has spawned it becomes what is known as a kelt. Most kelts remain in fresh water until the spring, when they return to the estuaries. There they feed well on

---

* In other localities the finnock is known as 'blackneb' and 'herling'. The official term is 'whitling', but this is confusing since on the Tweed 'whitling' refers to sea trout of 1–2½lb, while fish under 1lb are known as 'black-tails'. The finnock is to the sea trout as the grilse is to the salmon.

the elvers which are just coming into the estuaries at that time. In April it is rather difficult to distinguish an estuary sea trout kelt from a clean-run fish merely by the shape. The kelt is normally very thin, but after feeding on elvers for a very short time, even just a day or two, it gets a good shape, though the flesh is pale, condition is poor, and it has still got the distinctive black back and black cap.

Sea trout can live a long time and they return to the waters of their youth year after year and spawn many times. Because of this it is essential that great care is taken not to injure a kelt when it is caught.

In rivers and lochs, however, a kelt is easily recognised. It is long and thin and its head looks disproportionately large. It has hard, prominent teeth. The silvery appearance is rather dead and pearly, the back is black and the line of demarcation between the black and the silver is very distinctive. The head has a black cap and this black cap is the last kelt appearance to leave the sea trout. It would seem to vanish as the sea trout's condition becomes more that of a 'clean' fish, and I do not mean by 'condition' merely the contours of the fish, which can be so misleading.

The drainage of moors and hills has led to an upturn in the incidence of 'flash' spates which destroy many redds and much feeding. The great areas now under afforestation take up a high percentage of the water table and, in near drought conditions, leave streams very low in places and non-existent in others. The fry and young fish fare badly and the solitary heron and gregarious seagulls well.

For Reference

G. H. NIALL's book *The Life of the Seatrout* (Seeley Service, 1930), 400-odd pages long and including more than a hundred plates and illustrations, remains a book of tremendous interest to all fishermen. I cannot attempt to tell the life of a great fish in a few pages but it is a life I have been concerned with for nearly sixty years, dating, I'm sure, from 1928, when I captured the oldest recorded sea trout – a beautiful fish of 12½lb, eighteen and a half years old, which had spawned eleven times. The following year I caught another of my largest sea trout. It was 14lb but as it was only twelve years old there was nothing very noteworthy about its life.

I am indebted to Mr Andy Walker, of the Freshwater Fisheries Laboratory, Pitlochry, for the following information in 1984.

Your fish of eighteen and a half years remains the oldest recorded rod-caught sea trout in the UK. However, Ian Hynd and I have had scales from fish with as many spawn marks and the greatest number was shown by a fish taken by netting below Loch Stack in 1964* (2.1+13sm+). Pertinent to this, it is not always the largest fish which prove to be the oldest and have the largest number of spawning marks. The oldest found among eleven hundred sets of scales from Lochs Maree, Clair and Coulin in 1980 was a 3.0+11sm+, yet it weighed only 3¼lb!

The Tweed is a prolific source of big, fast-growing, short-lived sea trout, commonly maiden two sea-winter fish. Rarely do we encounter fish with more than one or two spawning marks there, so they are much younger than the big sea trout of the north-west.

*2.1+13sm+ denotes two fresh-water winters before going to sea, one maiden winter in the sea, and thirteen spawning marks plus one dire.

A point which emerges from *The Statistical Bulletin* issued by the Department of Agriculture and Fisheries (April 1984), which lists recorded catches from salmon fisheries, is that the weight of sea trout caught was 25 per cent less than in 1981 but 5 per cent up on the average for the ten years from 1971 to 1981.

2

SEA TROUT IN RIVERS

WHEN the sea trout leave the estuaries, they move into a river either to reside in it or as a route to the loch above it. In the spring, the fish are usually large and comparatively few in number, though in some rivers, for example the Tweed and the Beauly, as well as in the many estuaries round the coasts where there is such luscious winter feeding, great numbers of fish of finnock size or a little larger are caught.

In the rivers which have an abundance of these early runs

fishing is with fly, worm and spinner. In those where only a few heavy fish come in, there are many problems and, unfortunately, the productive period is too short and the fish too scarce to make any serious experiment possible. These small runs of sea trout seem to occur particularly in those rivers which do not have large runs of spring salmon, and because of this it is frequently possible to get permission to fish for them in strictly preserved waters.

Fishing the Spring Run

THE fish are rather unpredictable. I have caught them in small, fast-running pools with size 5/0 salmon flies, as well as in nice streams with a size 8 sea trout fly. Generally, it can be assumed that these rivers and waters are all for fly fishing only. One particular river I know well has a dam built on it to form an artificial pool. When the temperatures are low (as they normally are in April) the fast outflows, especially the nasty, rough and rugged water below the dam, which is so unattractive in waters below 6°C may stop the fish from running – not only the sea trout but the salmon too. This has its advantages, because in the clear pool below the dam every fish can be seen. The first salmon and then the first sea trout arrive and the pool begins to fill up with fish. I have observed between twenty and thirty salmon and from fifteen to twenty sea trout in it at the one time. One of these sea trout was approaching 20lb in weight – at least, that was my estimate. This happens year after year, and it was of interest to have a visually accurate guide to the numbers in these runs. There is no doubt that the cold, turbulent water deterred the fish, and the complete absence of catches or any indication of fish further upstream seems to confirm this. I caught a few of these fish, but did not find any particular method I'd say was best. The heaviest weighed 12½lb. It was possible to fish this pool from a high south bank and see both the fly's action and the response of the fish. Few sea trout showed any interest. The fact that the fish met an obstruction and slipped back into the pool seemed to put them completely off the take, particularly the salmon.

By way of contrast, on another river not at all famous for its sea trout, I recall one bright, sunny day in May when the water was slightly below a good size and I was fishing for salmon. A splash at the tail of the pool caught my eye and I went back up a fairly high bank and downstream to above where the fish had shown. There, in what looked like six inches of water, lay the fish. The water depth was probably nearer three or four feet, but in the gin-clear water and sunshine, with every detail of the clean, stony bottom intensely clear, the fish was so distinct that it seemed magnified many times. To have seen a salmon would have been interesting, but to see a sea trout of 8 or 9lb, looking as only a silver fish straight out of the sea can look, was really something.

The fish appeared to be quite settled, although it can only just have arrived in the pool as it was not there when I passed up to the neck of the pool a few minutes earlier. There was no mistaking it for a salmon. The head, the spots, the thickness of the wrist above the tail, the square tail itself – all could belong only to a sea trout.

When I go out for an hour's fishing I take only my rod, reel, line and a cast of flies, plus whatever flies may be behind the lapel of my jacket, and so it was on this occasion. I had on a 9lb breaking strain cast with a Grouse and Claret Blue Hackle on the top dropper, a Cinnamon and Gold in the middle (both size 8), and a size 4 Silver Doctor on the tail. What appeared to be the best of my limited selection was a size 6 Jock Scott instead of the rather large Silver Doctor, which I was sure would have frightened the fish. I put on the Jock Scott, kept well upstream and cast a long line far downstream at about 45° and let the fly swing round in a smooth, slow glide a few yards above the fish. All looked well. The next cast I brought the fly round just in front of the fish and it took the Jock Scott as fast and as furiously as any take I have ever seen. I won the ensuing battle, and my catch proved to be an 8½lb sea trout covered with sea lice in a pool about a mile and a half from the sea.

The capture of such a fish with such tackle has not come my way again – perhaps because I do not usually risk offending fish by using such a cast specifically for sea trout, but I use it so often for salmon that the chance of taking a sea trout is usually there. It does show what can happen, but I would like it to happen fairly frequently and predictably before I would take this as universally acceptable tackle for sea trout. A method of fishing or an opinion on the effects of thickness of nylon cast and fly size cannot be justified if based only on a few captures or losses.

Fastidious Sea Trout

THE large spring sea trout which are not captured in the spring remain to be caught in the pools in June, when they really do take, as long as their fastidiousness is really appreciated and catered for. These fish provide a great attraction before the main runs of sea trout begin to come in. I know of several rivers where a variety of pools will hold heavy fish every year and they all seem to offer at least one chance of being caught. If that chance is missed, however, the prospect of success is minimal. Very occasionally such fish are caught during the day. The biggest I have seen weighed 14½lb, and it was caught in fresh water at the neck of a shallow pool in water four or five feet deep. It is usually better to leave such fish undisturbed during the day and fish for them at night. We shall be thinking about them again when we discuss night fishing.

Usually the first runs of sea trout are of fairly large fish, with few of less than 2½lb. Where they are running through it is sometimes difficult to catch them. In a large, short river where great numbers are running, most well-defined pools are good from the very neck to the draw-away at the pool's tail, and there are usually fish in the water, so that a rise to the fly may come at any cast.

Strangely, in smaller rivers the running fish do not take well in all pools, only in specific ones, and they prove to be the same ones year after year. I do not mean that *no* fish will take elsewhere – odd ones may be caught in the strangest of places and in the strangest of ways – but these particular pools are the best taking pools. Whether it is that they provide good lies or allow the fish time to be distracted, I don't know. It is not their distance from the sea or the loch that makes them the best taking pools, nor do they appear to be pools where fish habitually rest.

The Lessons of One Pool

IN one particular river which was part of the hotel water there were several pools where fish took well and others which were useless, though perfect to look at. The best pools gave great opportunities. Some guests would accept advice and stay at one of the better pools, and, if fishers at all, would get good baskets. Others who preferred to fish down all the scenic pools seldom achieved much – other than recreation of their spirits. This was during the months of July and August and didn't apply quite as much during September.

The best method was to keep fishing the fly down one particular pool as there were always odd fish passing through which at least offered a chance. Not all the fish that went through the pool showed, but if you sat and watched the pool, particularly the tail, fish would often break the surface as they came into the pool. As soon as a fish showed we started fishing at the best taking part of the pool and fished down slowly to the tail, catching what one could from the run. A dash back to the neck of the pool might yield another fish before the run had completely passed through. Another energetic dash to the pool above might give another meeting with the run, but this presented a problem never satisfactorily solved. By the time the upper pool was reached, the fish might already have passed it, or they might not have reached it. What was happening at the pool below? Ah, the glorious uncertainty of fishing!

This was a spate river and the fish ran it only when there had been some rain and it was from half a foot to four feet above summer level. The best cast was a Heckham and Black on the top dropper, a Grouse and Claret on the middle, and a Peter Ross on the tail. They were all size 8 on 8lb breaking strength nylon, or, in clear conditions, 6lb breaking strength. In September, it's interesting to recall, we never used the Grouse and Claret or a Dunkeld because it invariably meant the hooking of a salmon and, though we may wonder at a salmon fisher despising sea trout, we mustn't forget that a salmon can ruin a day's sea trout fishing, or much of it. Who wants a salmon when there are good sea trout about, anyway?

Taking Pools

WITHOUT local knowledge it takes a little time and study to find the taking pools in such a river. Sometimes there are long gaps between the runs, as often happens with heavy spates, and the right pool might be a pretty dull place when you are uncertain whether or not it *is* the right pool in the first place. Such pools are easier to identify during a small spate, when it is especially necessary to do so because the fish run through fast then and do not take well anywhere, and the only real chance is in these pools. Every river has its own best size for fishing and knowing this size is essential for success. A river fishes best when its best size is reached after a heavy spate rather than a small one.

When the river in question was fished down from pool to pool, the chance of meeting fish in one of the taking pools was so greatly reduced that sport was poor. Indeed, for many years the river has been reported as 'going back', and not being nearly so good as in days of old. But I have fished it only once in the last twenty-odd years and found it as good as ever. Of course, many rivers have 'gone back' because of hydroelectric schemes and pollution, though hydroelectric schemes have been blamed unjustly in some cases. Floods, too, have done irreparable damage.

Fishing Late and Early

SEA trout which are lying and settled in a river seldom rise to the wet fly during the daytime. Indeed, when such fish appear to rise it is possible that they are really running fish, in the sense that they are moving – perhaps not from the sea to the loch at the head of the river, but merely from one lie to another, albeit a few pools upstream. It is not until dusk that they begin to rise freely in any way, first to the natural fly and then to the artificial fly if it is properly presented to them. They continue to rise to the latter long after complete darkness has crept up from the valleys below.

I have heard of the wonderful way fish rise and take before sunrise, but somehow this is not a time of day I like to fish. I have fished at this time on many occasions, and with varied results, as a continuation of my night fishing, particularly when that has not been a success because of the earlier disturbance of the fish. However, even when I have made a special pre-dawn expedition I have not enjoyed success commensurate with the effort expended. Not so with salmon. When fishing in the thin shadow of a rock or tree, I have caught salmon in lies right up to the last minute before the sun ruined all in the very low water. Indeed, using the same kind of shade from the moon has given me many sea trout in lochs as well as in rivers.

Day Rises

IN many pools, shallow as well as deep, great numbers of large sea trout may be seen during the daytime. Some may even be seen rising slowly from the deep of a still pool, making only a tiny ring on the surface. Doubtless these fish are taking something on the surface or from just under it, though they don't even appear to open their mouths. It's as though they are pushing their noses up just enough to break the surface tension of the water. I have not seen them take anything artificial with any regularity, although I have seen all sorts of 'things' offered to them and in all sorts of ways. The nearest I can claim to any success with them has been in the late evening but before the natural rise – when strictly they should be left completely undisturbed to be certain of success later.

Frequently, I have caught them on a tiny size 16 Dunkeld on 4lb breaking strain nylon. My heaviest so far has been 7½lb. It is a satisfactory method of fishing in many ways, but as this tackle is too fine for such fish I certainly don't use it except with the long rod and fine line. It doesn't take long to kill a fish with this tackle, but striking the tiniest of snags can be disastrous. At dusk and darkness, most of these fish slip back to the tail of the pool, or to the shallow banks in the pool, or even, on occasion, up into the neck of the pool – and they do fish well then.

This brings to my mind a vivid picture of a pool half a mile from home when the river was low and full of sea trout. My father was with me and we were sitting on a bank high above the pool with a perfect view of the fish in the sunlight. They were coming up to the surface and making the tiny rings that we'd seen so often. Naturally, the talk was of what we could do to get these fish in daytime. We had a good idea about what to do at night, but daylight presented difficulties we hadn't solved. Even now it seems that I'll never know the answer.

In the midst of this great number of fish ranging from 1½ to 7 or 8lb was a fish of over 10lb, easily the heaviest fish of the run. My father and I agreed that it was a very desirable fish. I went down to one of the lowest pools in the river – a pool that I knew was full of heavy fish, and one which I liked even though it was a three-mile walk downstream. At that time petrol was rationed and there were no cars; indeed, there was no road to cycle on. The pool came up to my expectations all right and I stopped fishing when I had almost too much to carry. The problem was, should I wait and get all that I could at that pool or should I leave space as well as strength for the big one in the pool nearer home which we'd been admiring earlier? It would be dreadful if I couldn't carry it home! So I left the space and reserved the energy.

Such is my optimism and such is my luck always with sea trout.

I rose but one fish and caught it. It was 10¾lb, and from its absence from the upper pool it seemed that I had caught just that one out of the vast numbers in the pool. Then, of course, I had no intention of catching anything else. Just that big one!

How easily I could be convinced of the existence of some sort of power of mind over fish, so often has this happened to me and, indeed, so often have I anticipated it aloud and then demonstrated it to others. To some extent I think that this might result from my knowledge of perfect conditions, but that would not account for the take of the one large fish. If there were two fish lying side by side in a pool and I caught one of them, then it would be the larger of the two. My late brother, who was as good a fisher if not a better fisher than I, would get the smaller one. Of course, I *knew* I was going to get the larger one. He only *hoped* to get the larger!

Fishing a Falling Water

A FALLING water after a heavy spate gives the best sport, probably because the fish can travel slowly and without fear of being stranded in small pools. By good sport I do not mean catches of finnock, which you should put back, or only one or two sea trout, but baskets of from ten to twenty sea trout averaging 2lb or so. This is not the class of catch reserved for what I have heard described as 'a tiny coterie of pundits', who go fishing for a short time on expensive waters every August. There is quite a lot of my kind of fishing still to be found at a reasonable cost, but it has to be looked for. If I mentioned some of it here it would become over-crowded and over-disturbed in a very short space of time. No, I think that the gems should be found – and, once found, treasured.

Wet Fly Technique

WHEN fishing the pool, cast across and slightly downstream – about 30°. Let the fly swing round across the pool without slipping back downstream. Do not strike a sea trout, just tighten. The stream keeps the line fairly taut and it is all too easy to strike too quickly. The flies are comparatively small and hooks should be sharp so that they penetrate quite easily. Sea trout which are fresh in from the sea are very soft in the mouth and if you're heavy-handed in playing them the hook can cut clean through its hold. A cardinal rule: don't be too hard when playing them.

The use of the top dropper on the surface will yield sea trout when no other method of fly fishing will. In order to fish that dropper in the most effective way, a twelve foot rod and light line are essential. It is difficult to cast with at the beginning but once the technique is mastered casting distances do not suffer. This can be quite demanding on the fisher, but nothing worth mastering is easily done. Care is also needed in matching the strain you put on the fish to the strength of the nylon used, but one doesn't need many reminders about that. It is a lesson quickly learned.

With a cast of three flies the tail fly fishes like a single fly. It can be made to sink a little deeper if so wished, and can produce results equal to a single fly, which is sometimes difficult to get below the surface of a fast stream with a short line.

The middle fly comes nearer the surface and is, in a way, a perfect guide to whether or not the leader is too heavy. Fish always seem to rise short to it if the nylon is too thick.

Fish will come short to the tail fly too if the cast is too heavy, but the reason for the short rise is not so obvious. It might be due to the size of the fly, or the speed at which it is fished. The top dropper, however, can bring great results. Draw it across the surface at right angles to the stream and it will rise fish which will not usually come to a sunk fly fished in the usual manner. If the fish misses a fly, it will almost certainly rise again until it is hooked or has touched the fly or cast or has been disturbed for some other reason.

Dropper and Bob Fly Methods

WHEN I say draw the bob fly across the stream I mean bring the fly across so that it makes a steady wave against the stream – the steady wave a quarter-submerged fly makes, not the disturbing drag made by an almost completely sunk fly when, for example, it is not tied on properly and hangs obliquely instead of straight. A dropper treated with a proprietary dry fly solution is not successful. It is just as useless, I believe, as allowing your fly to drag when fished dry in the approved manner. It produces a bubbly effect which is neither what is wanted nor desirable.

An upstream wind is a great asset. It helps to get the bob

fly up as well as much farther across the pool or stream than is otherwise possible. It also prevents the flies from slipping back with the current, which in itself can mean poor results. The upstream wind produces quite a belly in the line, but this is a help in hooking fish which rise to the bob. The middle and tail flies give the weight necessary to fish the bob effectively and they themselves continue to fish in a proper and attractive manner. With only two flies on the cast, the top fly does not seem to me to fish effectively, either in a loch or on a river.

The bob fly is also effective when fished across the glide from side to side of the stream and to the very edge of the river – if possible from the far side of the stream, since on occasions sea trout run very close to the side.

Plucking at the Fly

SOMETIMES the touch of a sea trout can be very deceptive, particularly if the cast is too thick. The overall effect the fisher experiences – or *thinks* he is experiencing – is that he has been touched by a small trout. The most striking example of this occurred a good many years ago. My father had advised a guest to fish at a particular pool in the river. The water was perhaps a little on the low side and the day was light with high cloud but no direct sunshine. The little-experienced guest may well have had an opinion of his own, wanting to go out elsewhere, but with greater experience he would have taken the advice willingly. But this one halted between the two and went down to the recommended pool with rather mixed feelings and returned at lunch time to report that it was of no use and that he had touched nothing but parr. Although this happened a long time ago, I distinctly remember that he was quite peeved and went away to fish in the loch and without glory. The irritation was not only on his side.

My father told me to go down and fish the pool since there was obviously a run of big fish in it. I did not need to be told twice. The outcome was dramatic. I got one or two touches as soon as I started fishing. The excitement within me was high, I can tell you. I steadied myself and drew the flies very slowly in the barely moving current. The expected touch came and I eased all towards it at the very moment of the touch and then tightened. This happened twice and I had two sea trout, one of 6½lb and one of 7½lb. Then all went dead, so I headed for home, recalling that a few years previously it was at that very pool that at seven o'clock one morning before school, and all alone, I had caught my first salmon. I had risen the salmon twice, and its capture, after rising the second time, was wonderful. I wasn't able to carry both rod and fish, all 14lb, so I left my rod, reckoning no doubt that I could get another in time, but never again my first salmon. I staggered delightedly up the path home.

My father was not in the least surprised to see me with the two sea trout which the guest had unwittingly spurned. He said that the run would have moved on and that it would probably be in a small pool or stream a mile further up by about tea time.

I kept the second appointment and got one on the bob in the fast stream. I can see it rise yet. I have a photographic memory for rises, but, alas, for little else. In the small pool I had another lovely rise and had two sea trout to take home, one of 5½lb and the other of 8½lb. My father showed a little satisfaction and, no doubt, felt a lot, but I didn't sense the full glory as I'm sure that he would have caught twice as many.

An Unforgettable Day

THAT particular guest did not take the lesson to heart as he should have done. A few years later there was a somewhat similar happening, except that on this occasion he would go neither to the river nor, as was suggested also, to the loch. Instead he went to his own choice, a little river seventeen miles away. However, my brother took my father's advice and went to the loch recommended and there he had one of his best days ever, fifteen or twenty sea trout. I forget the exact number, but he had a wonderful basket. I went to the river as suggested. It was one of those days I recall with bowed head. I made a dreadful mess of it.

The stream was full of huge fish when I started, and panic seized me. Each rise I struck too hard and with an increasing frenzy. Suffice it to say that my cast, my only cast (I had forgotten everything else) was reduced to eighteen inches in length and the only fly I had left was a size 4 Jock Scott (the equivalent of today's size 11) and it was a battered old fly. This short cast needed extra care in fishing – not only because of the difficulty of casting it but also because, since it was my last little length of cast, if that went all was lost.

However, success did come my way in the form of a lovely 9lb sea trout. When I had landed it the pool seemed empty, and probably it was. As I raced up to a small lie amongst trees I pictured the run of fish heading upstream with some of its members adorned with my flies. There was really little chance of my being able to land a fish in that particular spot, but I'm afraid that I didn't think of that at the time, and I didn't care either. I wanted to meet those fish again. On the second cast I hooked another heavy fish, but as it turned downstream through rocks and into white water I was broken before I really knew what was what. I felt rather sad about it all.

Light, Polaroids and Reactolites

LIGHT is as important on a river as on the loch. It is perfect when it is as one sees it through Polaroid or Reactolite glasses. I don't like wearing them because I don't like fishing under conditions which appear to be perfect all the time. Variations in light are important to me in my fishing and I cannot detect them while wearing these glasses.

Another reason for not liking them when I'm fishing a river is that they make it so easy to see fish in the pools that one is tempted to go and have a look before actually fishing. This is the wrong thing to do, because before actually fishing. This is the wrong thing to do, because a stale fish might easily be disturbed and if it careers around the pool it could well disturb a clean fish, making it rise short. In addition, as you approach a pool to look at it with Polaroids on you are in fact very much nearer to it than you realise. When you take them off and look at the pool, there is the awful realisation that you are standing in a most conspicuous position – a position you would normally never find yourself in were you taking the usual care. Furthermore, if one has a tendency to strike a little too soon, Polaroids are not at all helpful, because one sees the fish earlier in its rise and the real danger is that the fly will be drawn away before the fish can take it.

I do, however, think that it may be wise to wear Polaroids in order to absorb the strong light reflected from the water as well as a safety measure. The wind can play tricks with a fly and sight is precious to a fisherman.

— 3 —

SEA TROUT IN LOCHS

A GREAT deal of my experience with sea trout has centred on lochs. By the greatest good chance I was brought up on the shores of Loch Maree, and most anglers will at once realise what that means. Maree is among the finest of sea trout lochs both for the numbers of fish as well as for their quality. Every season it yields a prodigious number of sea trout to wet fly and the dap. Maree has produced the largest sea trout to be taken in a loch, a magnificent fish of 19½lb caught by Mr David C. McNaught in 1951. Other fish have been caught close to this mark on other waters I know well. Loch Hope has produced at least one of 18lb; Loch Eilt has given another of 17lb.

Again I quote Andy Walker, writing in 1984:

> The current British rod-caught record sea trout is one of 20lb and possibly an ounce or two, caught last autumn in the Tweed at Peebles by George Leavy. It was taken on 1½-inch silver and black tube fly. The former record 22½lb River Frome fish was not reinstated when the British Rod-caught Record Fish Committee a few years ago drew up its code of procedures for establishing records.
>
> We can cite a number of big fish caught by netting, including one of 26lb 2oz caught on 18 July 1974 on the River Echaig and weighed by Ian Hynd. Its weight on capture almost two days earlier was said to have been 28½lb. One of 23½lb was taken at Berwick-on-Tweed on 16 July 1963, and another of the same weight at Achiltibuie in April 1963. One of over 21lb was caught in the Tweed sweep nets in 1982, so there are still some about.

It is not only on the larger lochs that we can look for sea trout fishing of quality. Many of the smaller waters of Scotland, both on the mainland as well as in the Hebrides, give magnificent fishing. We shall, however, discuss the techniques of loch fishing in general and in such a way that the angler who follows them, whether on a large or small loch, will have the maximum chance of success.

Approaching a Loch

A LOCH can be a rather daunting sight to a beginner or to someone new to its waters. Where are the fish in all the acres of water? I shall try to show later in this chapter, by example as well as reminiscence, how sea trout drifts must be discovered and studied before fish can be taken. Certainly, the angler should never drift about aimlessly hoping for fish. He should think about his drifts and, if possible, cover water between six and twenty feet in depth. But I will begin with the problem which irritates most anglers – short rising.

Short Rising

ON a number of occasions anglers return at night with tales of fish rising short, rising just as the flies were being lifted off the water for the next cast, or, worse than that, often of no fish, or very few, having been risen, and – I've heard it so often – 'There are no fish in the loch'. Sometimes, it is true, there are no fish to be seen showing themselves, but the reasons for the non-taking risers are the same, year after year after year – drawing the flies through the water too quickly, for too short a time, or fishing with a long line and drawing it in so slowly that rising fish are not seen. This is what happens when a short rod and a heavy line are used by any but a very small band of experts.

Sea trout take late in the cast. If, for example, the duration of drawing the fly through the water for brown trout on a normal free-rising day is to the count of five, then the duration of fishing the cast for sea trout should be to the count of ten – at least. They usually rise any time from the count of five to the end of the cast, even to under the very gunwale of the boat, hence the numerous short rises many anglers encounter when fishing too quickly. I make allowances for the fish which follow the fly slowly and only show up when it is speeded up as the back cast is started and cannot be satisfactorily stopped.

Drawbacks of a Long Line

THE apparent solution is to cast a long line and draw it in slowly, but this is not really the answer – not even for an angler with fair experience. There is a lot of line in the water, the flies are well sunk even when the line is greased unless drawn quickly, and satisfactory contact with the flies is lost. Much line has to be brought in by hand to neutralise the speed at which the boat is drifting onto the flies, and faster handlining is called for to keep the flies moving. A coil of line, or all sorts of coils of line on your knees or in the bottom of the boat, round a button or the rod end or the handle of a landing net, is not the best state of preparedness for hooking a 5lb sea trout.

There are many dangers in handlining when fishing from a boat. Only the expert can master them. The angler who fishes a long line usually reports a few rises, but in most cases the fact of the matter is that he gets many rises and is quite unaware of them because he is unable to spot a boil from a fish in a breeze, no matter how light the breeze. There are many degrees of boils. They vary from the faint sign of the fish which has turned slowly to the cartwheel of a heavy fish turning quickly and fairly deep. I have often seen and been told of the cartwheel being undetected, but it is perhaps not easy when one doesn't know exactly what to look for.

It is extremely difficult to see the line 'going' as it does when a fish takes a fly fished on a long line. In such cases the strike must be made very quickly. By the line 'going' I mean that the slight belly in the line between the rod tip and the water straightens a little, but nothing is felt. Even when a fish gives a pull it is often undetected by the inexperienced. I have often seen a rod tip bend slightly with the pull of a fish but been assured that the fish did not touch the fly – and it's not always the inexperienced who fail to detect what's happening.

Advantage of a long rod. The bob fly
works for longer on the surface.

Advantage of a Long Rod

THE long rod and light line make fishing the bob fly easy. It is almost impossible with a short rod and a heavy line and never really satisfactory, in spite of great efforts to make it so. It is easy to cast the comparatively short distance required from a boat. After making the cast, pause for a count of, say, four before raising the rod point slowly to bring the top dropper steadily along the surface for the last third of the cast. The last yard or so of the line may be drawn in by hand, so as to avoid having to bring the rod point too far back. The danger in bringing it back too far is that the line falls close to the rod end and when a fish has risen and been struck the angle of pull on the rod can sometimes be so acute that the rod tip is almost assuredly broken or severely strained.

Breeze

THE breeze is important. A soft ripple on the surface is the favourite of many and is good at night. Nevertheless, a steady wind which produces a good wave is best of all. A 'good wave' is a wave whose rocking motion doesn't make sitting in a boat uncomfortable. A gusty wind is not good, but preferable to a glassy calm. The west wind is the one we call the best, and usually it is, but on many lochs it can also be the worst – for example on some of the lochs which run north and south and have awkward hills nearby, which play all sorts of tricks with what would normally be a steady breeze. Here a north or east wind is often best. The afternoon 'sea breeze' we get in most areas is disappointing, as it's seldom good at the start and produces the best results just as it is fading away.

When the breeze is light or even in a dead calm, a longish line should be cast and the line drawn in very slowly after an even longer pause than usual, and the bob should not be raised to the surface. The light line shows a take much more distinctly than a heavy line. This take is not as difficult to detect as when fishing a river, for in the river the effects of the currents can be considerable.

Quiet Takes

IN sea trout fishing one of the most difficult facts to comprehend is that a fish can take the fly properly and yet not be felt. The line goes out or, rather, straightens slightly but nothing is felt, possibly because the fish rises, takes the fly and continues slowly in the direction of the boat. A call from the ghillie is unlikely to allow for the strike to be made in time and, indeed, his call often brings the reply that the fish has missed the fly. So be it, but the ghillie usually knows – particularly if he is sufficiently interested to call in the first place – and, also, he can see much more than the less experienced fisherman and his view of the water is from a different angle.

The bob fly fished properly on the surface, at the right time, adds 30 per cent to the number of rises produced by fishing with sunk flies only and about 20 per cent to the number of fish caught. It gives all the results of the wet fly and more than most of the advantages of dapping. However, let me give a word of warning. Do not put dry fly floatant such as Mucilin on the bob in an attempt to make it fish more easily. The idea is attractive and fish are occasionally caught, but it produces a stream of bubbles and is not usually a success. An oiled bob fly doesn't answer the idea behind dropper fishing and does not truly represent the stage of transition from a hatching nymph to a fly on the surface, nor does it simulate the insect flying away from the water.

Choice of Fly

FAVOURITE flies for daytime fishing differ from loch to loch, but not as much as might be expected, and the Black Pennell, Soldier Palmer, Kate McLaren [named after the author's mother – see Appendix 1, p. 153], Invicta, Grouse and Claret, Pennell and Claret, Peter Ross and Teal Blue and Silver would provide the basis of a good three-fly cast for any loch. The sizes are usually 8s but a number of lochs need size 6 in a decent breeze. Size 10 is recommended on many lochs but my experience leads me to believe that this is too small for best results.

Striking

THERE is no controversy about striking when fishing from a boat. Almost always strike, but in the knowledge that almost every separate rise has its own correct time for the strike. One can go from the immediate strike to the long wait for a head-and-tail rise, or – seemingly quite ridiculous – to no strike at all, as when a fish misses a fly and the flies are drawn on until the fish rises a second or third time or more, or takes or touches a fly, all in one draw of the cast.

I cannot attempt to detail all the types of rises and times to strike (nor, indeed, might it be wise to) but one other rise which must be mentioned is when only the boil on the surface is seen – and it is not always easy to see, as I have already remarked. Strike as soon as the boil is seen. The fish has already turned away. A risen fish, if untouched, will almost certainly rise again, so get the flies into the water and over the fish as quickly as you can. In fact fish often seem to wait on or very near the surface looking for the fly, particularly if they have risen to the bob. Anglers who fish the bob as well as those who dap will have seen this happen frequently. Remember that the boat is drifting onto the fish. There is no time to waste. A sea trout is waiting for you!

Sea Trout Lies in Lochs

THE sea trout loch presents many problems until the lies are known. Unless guidance is gleaned from some source, the loch may not provide much sport. The main river mouth, the burn mouths, the points, the banks of weeds, the islands and the general appearance of the loch and its shores are all guides to where to fish, but are no real indication of the best lies.

Sea trout do have favourite lies and I know many on lochs and even what size of fish can be expected from each lie. The fact that we may find and rise a fish anywhere adds to the pleasures of anticipation, but remember that any lie can be missed by a yard or two, so chase after every scrap of information to be had from any source about where fish are seen to jump, where they are risen, caught or lost.

My memories take me back to the annual appearance of 2½lb fish in the same lie every year on the 4th or 5th of July in one loch I know well. It was a lie easily found by landmarks. Another lie I know in another loch seems impossible to pinpoint, yet my father did just that for me when he first showed it to me. It was on a terrific day, from start to finish, and I shall let myself recall it briefly.

Rain which had fallen on the day before we went to this particular loch had put both the river and the loch up and the fish were running. When we reached the loch at about 10.30a.m. it was like a mirror, with the high rugged hills reflected in its still surface, doubling their magnificence, which even I appreciated to the full. I had just been invalided out of the army at the time. I decided to fish the narrows where the river left the loch and, in spite of the lack of a breeze, this yielded four sea trout, the heaviest 10lb, as well as a 10lb salmon, all on a Peter Ross before midday. Exciting indeed, but the day was still young. At one point I saw great activity and excitement in the boat in which my father was searching for puffs of wind ruffling the surface at odd places on the loch. He had hooked and was playing a

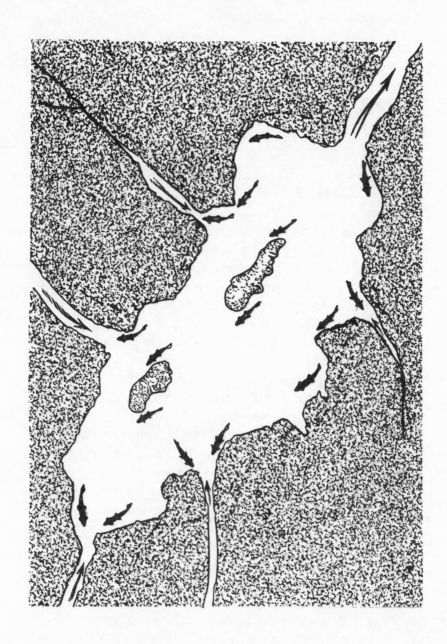

Typical sea trout lies in a loch.

good fish, which rolled round and round on the surface, finally breaking his cast. But it just lay there! The ghillie hurriedly backed the boat twenty yards or so and my father, who had put down his rod, quietly slipped the net under the fish – a lovely sea trout of 7½lb.

As usually happens, the fish held to their normal routes when running, so we both got into the boat when a breeze eventually came up about 2p.m. A particularly good fish, I remember now, came when we were 250 yards from the nearest shore or island. There was a perfect breeze and my father said that we would be coming to a good lie very soon. He had had a 10lb fish there two years before. He cautioned me that I would be at the spot in another few casts.

'Careful now! That's about it,' he said, and there and then I rose, hooked and landed a perfect specimen of sea trout weighing 11lb. My father's uncanny knowledge or fishing sense was proven again. I'd seen it so often before. But part of it might have been due to my infernal luck, which bothers me still from time to time.

We stopped fishing that day at 5p.m. with one salmon (10lb) and twenty-seven sea trout (116lb), the best being 11lb, 10lb, 7½lb, 6½lb, 6lb and 5lb, and all these had passed through extensive fishing available to the general public at low cost, though this particular loch was a private one. This was not a record day for that loch, but it was a memorable one. I shuddered to think what the disastrous effects might be if anything other than fly were permitted on this loch where I had such excellent sport.

In 1979 I did return and had shy rises from some good fish. My earlier fears were justified – spinning and worming of the river has been widely encouraged; even outboard engines were being used without the slightest regard for either the drifts or the fish. Today, when fish and good fishing are scarce commodities, surely extra care is needed. In the 'good old days' when there were plenty of sea trout, we were very quiet in the boat, taking great care to make sure that not even a wave from a rowed boat reached over the drifts contrary to the natural wave from the prevailing breeze. It we weren't very quiet then we knew about it by our lack of results.

Lines of Migration

AFTER entering the loch the sea trout usually fan out all over it and take up all the good lies. Many become almost permanent residents, remaining there until the urge to spawn drives them upstream to the redds. Others are merely temporary residents and quickly move on when they taste the fresh water after rainfall streaming down from the headwaters, a river, or another loch higher up the system. To that fresher water they move and may, indeed, feel at home until spawning time.

When the loch is low, the sea trout runs tend to move along the shoreline in a depth ranging from eight to fifteen feet of water. However, when the loch is high many hug the shoreline in much shallower water, sometimes not much deeper than four feet or so. To illustrate the perversity of the quarry, some are so intent on reaching the head of the loch that they run straight up the middle of it, swimming close to the surface. They take there, too. A watchful eye must be kept for jumping fish. Clean fish usually take. The black older residents are not quite so carefree.

When you meet a run of loch sea trout and drift over it, you may rise many fish and, if luck or expertise (or both) are in your boat, then a few may be caught. However difficult it may be, do resist the temptation to drift over that run again straight away. It isn't easy to resist but, if you can you will discover it is well worth the mental strain. Try to rest the drift for as long as possible – up to two hours, if you can stand it. If the run has moved on by that time, then, naturally, it will be a little further towards the head of the loch and, with care, you will find it again. Even fresh-run fish can be very easily disturbed and will come short if drifted over twice in quick succession.

Bear this in mind and remember also the very great wariness of fish which have been up for some time. On approaching a known good lie, stay clear of it if the conditions are not so good and there are reasonable expectations of an improvement before too long. The breeze may not be strong enough, or non-existent; the light on the water may be bad; or you may just suspect intuitively that something is not quite right. Wait for an improvement before going over the lie.

Light

THE light on the water is vitally important for success. It is at its best when it is exactly as it appears when viewed through Polaroids. I do not like wearing them because you are unable to detect the minute and important variations in the quality of the light on the water. These variations are very important to me, because I feel I know intuitively when the light is good and right and a fish will take. I think that it's quite natural that a little extra concentration should be invested in one's fishing at that particular time, for you know that the quality of the light is good, you know that the chances of a rise or rises are great, and therefore you are keyed up, your reactions are at their keenest and you are ready.

With Polaroids you don't see these changes in the quality of the light and you fish intently for a long, long time when the water appears to have a 'suitable' light. Then you get tired. There's a limit to the amount of adrenalin which can flow and so, when the light *is* right and a fish comes, you miss your chance. The only reason for recommending Polaroids would be to ease the strain on the eyes, but certainly not from the point of view of fishing.

Getting to Know a Loch

THE well-worn cliché 'Variety is the spice of life' doesn't apply to successful loch fishing. It is much better and much more satisfying to fish the same loch or lochs – knowing that they are good – until all the drifts, lies and runs of fish are engraved on your mind. It would take a lifetime of fishing a loch of any size for a fortnight a year before a fisherman could get to know it fully. Some drifts have only a two-yard width of good fishing down them. One rod can be over it, having great success, while the rod at the other end of the boat is having a depressingly dull time. I know of many places where half the length of the boat makes the difference between success and disappointment.

Often the drift is not straight, and keeping to the best fishing water entails moving in and out by shallow points jutting out from the shore and around clumps of weeds and weedbeds. If you allow the boat to drift straight you cross the best fishing only infrequently. I know of some drifts where the angler is advised to let the boat drift from one point to another and across the mouth of the bay between the two. There *is* a chance of a fish on the good water at the start of the first point, and then another chance after a long and dreary drift almost at its conclusion, just after drifting past the second point, and every now and again some running fish are met somewhere between the two points. This is enough to maintain the reputation of the recommended drift but fishing into the bays along the right depth contour would be much more productive.

On the smaller lochs of the Outer Hebrides the boat usually has a seat across the thwarts about a foot from the stern. The fisherman sits on the thwart and fishes out from the stern, covering an angle of 90°. His partner or the ghillie manoeuvres the boat in and out from the shore, around rocks and reefs, or around weedbeds. If a fish is risen and not hooked, a couple of very gentle and quiet pulls on the oars should enable the fisher to cover the rising fish two or three times, whereas the normal method of drifting with the wind and having two fishing, one close to the bow and the other in the stern, often means that the boat has drifted right over the rising fish before a second cast can be made. It does mean that the two fishermen take turn about on the oars, but it almost guarantees success.

Depth

IT is very difficult to get accurate information about the depths of a loch. An invaluable item of equipment to any sea trout angler – particularly since knowledge of depth is so vitally important – would be a simple and inexpensive depth sounder, rather than the clumsy and limited method of poking with an oar.

In my earlier days it was the knowledge of depths, lies and drifts that gave me so much good sport from lochs. Often I could not go out fishing until the evening, either because all the boats had been taken or it was the only time I could get away. I never fished the usual drifts, or, rather, the usual water drifted over. Instead, I took great care to follow the correct depth as I drifted down the shore or through a bay. In this way I covered much water that had been undisturbed during the day and was always able to pick up sea trout as I went along.

A very useful method of fishing the larger and more popular lochs is to arrange beforehand to fish early in the morning and later in the afternoon and into the evening and night. In this way the middle of the day is left free for sun-bathing, bird spotting or souvenir hunting with a non-fishing spouse and family.

When the boat is being rowed along between drifts it is a good plan, assuming your fellow angler is agreeable, to cast out to the side, preferably towards the shore, and to fish

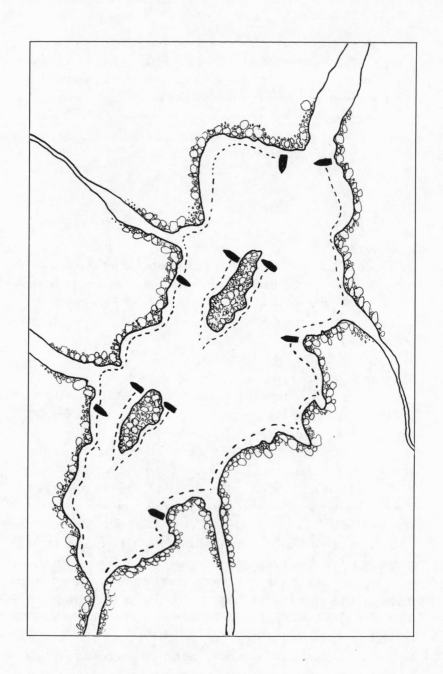

Fishing the loch shoreline correctly.

water that is considered hardly worth fishing but along which one has got to row. A great many fish can be picked up in this way but don't try it using an outboard engine. I learned of the hazards of that when I was very young. I had been casting with the outboard engine going when I hooked not a sea trout but a duck. Then I learned what would have happened had it been a good sea trout instead – the same chaos and the same disappointment, since the sea trout, like any self-respecting airborne duck finding itself hooked by a fisherman travelling in the opposite direction, will very speedily be lost.

4

Sea Pools, Estuaries and the Open Sea

Sea pools and estuaries can produce fish from April (or even earlier) until October, with, in my experience, a quiet time from mid-May onwards for about a month or so. In the seal-haunted voes of the Shetlands, the busy firths of the mainland estuaries and the curlew feeding-grounds of the sandy sea pools of the Hebrides, there is some time during every season when there is the opportunity of wonderful fishing. The exact time varies almost everywhere and the combined effects of drought or flood can have an effect on the timing, but the local angling clubs now springing up everywhere and so helpful to the visitor will provide reliable information. Should there be no such club in existence, then the local fishing-tackle supplier will help, even if he is fifty miles away. For the price of a drink or two in the local pub, ghillies or local fishermen are useful suppliers of inside knowledge. Tourist associations also publish information but, since this is generally about opening and closing dates rather than the best time for fishing, you should look for fishing booklets such as *Fishing in Sutherland*. This gives the characteristics of available fishings and where to find them and really is a most helpful publication. It would be for the benefit of all visitors to angling areas were every county to publish a similar booklet. Of course, reliable local information is the best of all, but we cannot escape the fact that it can be extremely difficult to obtain – perhaps by design. The individual may well be very jealous of his fishings, though, on the whole, I've found that he or she will give very valuable advice.

General Picture

IN the spring the early fish are on their way into the estuaries and kelts are on their way out. In summer the main runs are on their way in, with smaller numbers of fish passing through towards the end of the season. The best runs of fish are generally in June and July with a tapering off in August – except in the Shetlands, where the voes fish best in September. Estuary fishing is as affected by the weather as it is in the lochs of the mainland. High water in spring and during the arrival of the main summer runs tends to denude the sea pools of fish. Low water produces a great massing of fish which cannot run the rivers and consequently move in and out with the tide, often travelling miles along the coastline each time they go out, many of them characteristically hugging the coast within easy reach of the shore fishermen. In dry summers one can often find shoals of sea trout in sea lochs or brackish-water lochs, just lingering and waiting, like the fishermen, for welcome rain.

In certain areas where the lochs are very close to the sea it is common to find a shoal of sea trout present in the sea pools on one tide and on the next tide to discover that they have moved on. The absence of rain is not the only factor which will clear a sea pool of fish. The presence of a seal or seals will drive the sea trout back out of the pools to the comparative safety of the open sea. During or just after a period of stormy weather one tends to find seals sheltering in the relatively calmer waters of the sea pools and estuaries. It is now on record that in what was the worst year for returns from Loch Maree, 1987, there was a direct correlation between the poor returns and the presence of seals as far up as Kinlochewe.

Elvers

IN the spring the estuaries are, for a time, full of elvers, which are young eels two inches or so long which have travelled from their birthplace in the Sargasso Sea to the rivers. Having reached them, they ascend, but unlike the sea trout they live there for a few years as eels before making their long journey westwards into the setting sun to spawn and die. The run of large spring sea trout appears to come at the same time as the arrival of the elvers, and the descending kelts are seldom late in arriving on the scene.

Both fresh fish and kelts simply gorge themselves on elvers. The clean fish are usually large, 8–12lb, and don't stay long in the sea pool. However, while they are there, they will take. The problem is what and when. I have watched them break the surface of the water, dorsal fin completely ex-

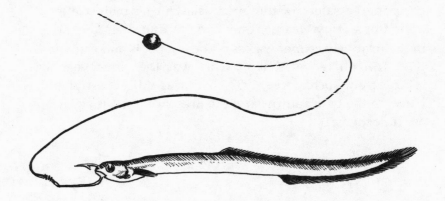

Mounting an elver.

posed. They splash and create great waves as they swim in the shallow water after the elvers or while seeking a taste of fresh water when the tide has been high and the river low. I have had them follow my bait close in to my feet without taking it – in fact, never coming closer to it than about eighteen inches. That has happened with the majority of my offerings – spinner, elver, sand-eel, terror and fly. Full tide is not really very successful, though I have caught fish in it and, indeed, in all states of the tide, but the best taking time seems to vary slightly in different districts. On average, I have found that half-tide and a short time either side of it is best of all. I tend to favour dusk, for fishing the sea pools, but half tide does not always occur at dusk. A terror is the easiest lure to fish at dusk and for me it has proved the most effective of all.

Large fish take the elver well during the day and, of course, at dusk, when fishing it is not at all easy unless the sea pool is small. Fish the elver with a spinning rod and fixed-spool reel with 8lb nylon, a little split shot about two feet from the hook, a size 12, which has been threaded through both jaws of the elver from the lower jaw up through the top one. This leaves the elver alive on the hook. Hooking the elver in the same way as a worm is not as successful. There is usually an abundance of elvers by the sea pool shore in April. If you lift a stone they are there in dozens. Scoop up a handful and they are back in the water, not in your hand. They are, as the cliché states, as slippery as eels. One fairly successful method is to shovel them with one hand into a handkerchief held in the other. Once there they are still not easy to hold and hook. A little fine sand does give some grip, but perhaps the best method is to put one on your trouser leg or kilt and then smack it once with the palm of the hand. This dries it a little and may also stun it – at least that's my thinking. After that treatment the task of impaling the tips of its jaws on to the hook is not difficult. Do remember that a dead elver is not a good bait.

Fishing the Bait

THE fish come in with the tide and are usually found in the rough water where the tide meets the current of the stream. This rough may be very slight indeed and even difficult to see with a downstream wind blowing. The shoal of fish often comes in, turns away, and goes back down the pool before heading up for another taste of the fresh water. It is not a good idea to follow them, or to try to do so. Cast the elver upstream and let it swing round in the current. Sometimes there may not be a fish near, but if there are any fish at all in the estuary they will come to you, so don't tire of this or be tempted to go further down, where they don't take as well. The main result will be that you disturb the fish, particularly if the day is bright. It is always worthwhile fishing every little corner, especially rough and white water and right up to the top of the sea pool. The head of the sea pool is the mark which separates the estuary from the fresh water at the height of the high tide. Unfortunately, in some cases, the river owners make the line of demarcation lower than this.*

Although the spring sea trout do not tend to lie at the head of the sea pools, being unpredictable, many odd ones do. Failing that, there is a very good chance of getting a large estuary trout.

Slob or Estuary Trout

THE estuary trout is a brown trout which has taken up residence in the sea pool area and thrives on the excellent feeding it finds there. In spite of their singularly unprepossessing nickname of 'slob' trout, I have seen them up to 14lb

* There are some sea pools where the fishing belongs to the local estate – T.G.L.

in weight, though 6lb is my own largest. It is difficult to tell the difference between a sea trout and an estuary trout when one takes the elver. Both do so with explosive ferocity and are off to sea on the first mad rush. Once the rush is weathered, all is as well as it can be when playing a large sea trout. My two heaviest sea trout from the estuaries were 8lb and 9lb and since neither of them came from the sea pools of rivers famed for their sea trout, this would suggest that they had just come in to taste the fresh water on their way along the coastline.

Kelts

EARLY in the year the estuaries tend to have large numbers of sea trout kelts making their way back to their feeding grounds. Many of them will be caught by the unwary. In both lochs and rivers, kelts are thin and lanky, but in the estuaries many of them are deceptively full. Some of them are in beautiful shape when caught, and not all of them can be reeled in like 'wet sacks' either, since they have begun to become reconditioned. The first real clue that all is not as it should be is the dull silver colour and the clear-cut line of demarcation between the silver body and the black back, so characteristic of the kelt. Some may, by this time, have only the black cap on the head. When handled they disgorge masses of elvers. This having been done, they reassume the kelt shape. Since the kelt sea trout is a particularly valuable fish – if not because it has perpetuated the species then because it may survive to return as an even larger fish – it does warrant careful treatment by way of a swift and gentle return to the water.

Fishing the sea pools early in the year can be a complete flop if the river is in full spate and the elvers are not massed together as in low water. The fish tend to lie away from the sea pools and there are so few 'clean' ones, as distinct from

63

The sea trout kelt.

kelts, that the task of looking for them along miles of unpromising coastline can be rather formidable and lacking in appeal unless one is happy with the estuary trout which are never far away.

Summer Runs

WHEN the main runs of sea trout come in during June, July and August, the actual degree of concentration of fish in the sea pools rather depends on the quantity of fresh water entering the sea. If the rivers are low, the fish congregate in the area, often moving in and out with each tide. One day the sea pool may appear to be full of fish but come the next day and they will have moved out again in search of fresh water elsewhere. It is not always guaranteed that a sea trout will return to its place of origin if there is no fresh water.

If the river is high enough for the fish to run up, they tend to do so without delay, and consequently the sea pool is full of fish only in so far as the runs pause on the way through. Indeed, sometimes the pause is so brief that there is doubt whether it exists at all.

There are nearly always finnock in most sea pools from June onwards until the end of the season, but it is best to return unharmed to the water any that are caught. These wee fellows give a degree of fun, but it is sea trout fishing that we are considering. Finnock are the grilse of the sea trout and they must be protected, since every one of them is a potential sea trout worth catching. Should fish of their size be wanted (for the cat or any other purpose) there is no shortage of lochs which would give comparable sport with brown trout, and their removal would do the lochs good. Whatever the degree of fun in catching these finnock, there is neither satisfaction nor glory in it, even though we do have evidence that they eat a considerable amount of ova at spawning time. I have no evidence before me to say that much of that ova might not have been waste material anyway.

In some estuaries there are good numbers of both finnock and sea trout present throughout the season, whether or not there are drought conditions. The fish may be coming into the estuary and then running straight upstream, so it is a case of knowing their usual route and trying to be in on it when they are passing through. It does seem to me that it is only during the few weeks of the main runs that this is really successful.

Tackle

A CAST of 6lb breaking strain, with three flies (size 10) usually produces results during the daytime. Peter Ross, Butcher, and Teal Blue and Silver are all good flies. Terrors and Demons are not as effective during the day, tending to come into their own at dusk, and it is better to fish these large lures singly. Silver and blue Devons, sand-eels, mackerel skin and Mepps spoons are good spinning baits in daylight and dusk, but putting aside the question whether or not spinners catch more fish than fly, the fly-caught sea trout is a very much greater prize than one caught by spinning. The skills involved give a greater sense of achievement – not, I hasten to add, because of any purism; it is just a matter of fact. The sea pool is not the place where the undoubted very high degree of skill needed for spinning under some conditions is required. Many of the Scottish firths, of course, give good sport to the spinner in areas far away from the river mouths.

For the sea pools I use a ten foot rod, a Hardy Perfect reel and a white floating line. In the dusk and dark an 8lb cast with two size 10 flies or one Badger Terror (which is my favourite of all the terrors) is a good choice. Should the pool be weedy or rocky, or if there is a wind blowing, then a single terror is best for many reasons, since it makes casting easier and it doesn't get entangled in the dark as can a cast of two or three flies.

Wading

WADING should be undertaken with the greatest of care. Seaweed is treacherous and when fishing it is not always easy to give due thought to the next step. A wetting is unpleasant, but skinning and bruising from the tiny rough barnacles and limpets which encrust the boulders of many estuaries is nasty and the abrasions and bruises cannot always be shown when recounting one's experiences.

Quicksands present another danger in estuary fishing. Always seek local information before fishing a sea pool for the first time. If you do get stuck, try to fall onto your back as gently as possible. With your feet and lower legs engulfed by the sand or bog, it is not as difficult as it sounds. The principle is to spread your weight as evenly as possible over the surface area of the sand. If you spread your arms out you will spread your weight more effectively.

Every movement from now on must be deliberately slow and gentle. The next stage is the release of your feet and legs. Again with very slow movements begin easing your feet and legs out of the sand or mud. If you try to pull quickly you will only create vacuums under your legs, which in turn will tend to pull you down deeper. Once your legs and feet are free (and this might take a quarter of an hour or more – for you *are* making every movement very slow and deliberate), it is relatively easy to begin to breast-stroke your way to firmer ground. (On a bog, use tussocks of grass or heather to pull yourself along). If you are still in contact with your rod or landing net or both, place the butt section of the rod or the net handle under your buttocks or the small of your back to assist with weight distribution.

It may take you an hour or two to reach firmer ground and you may have covered only a few yards' travelling distance – but it's worthwhile taking your time. Should you need a rest, just spread out your legs and arms as widely as possible. You will float in that position, even though it doesn't seem very secure.

Wind

It is interesting to find that in a great many estuaries an upstream wind is not the best at all. It tends to give a perfect appearance to the water. However, it remains one of the phenomena, not only baffling to me, but baffling to the locals who know the fishing, even if only in a set pattern, that a very light downstream breeze is best, but at night a dead calm is even better.

Speed of the Lure

Sea trout in brackish or salt water like a fairly fast-moving offering. However, a fly or spinner swinging round in a stream may be doing so quickly enough without additional rod movement or recovery of line by hand or reel. But as soon as it comes into slack water it must be kept moving by the angler. It is a common occurrence for many fish to be touched, risen, but not hooked – much to the angler's concern. He doesn't appreciate what happens when a fly is hurried round too quickly. A sea trout in the estuary or just out of salt water is very soft in the mouth and the fine wire of the fly hook or the triangle is easily pulled through the soft tissues of the mouth. This is when it is particularly important to lower your rod when the fish jumps. Great care must also be taken to avoid any harsh pulling on the fish for whatever reason. A heavy fly line can be a very great disadvantage with a fresh sea trout.

Moments of danger can also arise when bringing the fish in through or over weeds, so try to play it out completely beyond the weeds. A sign of a played-out fish is when it begins to wallow or roll on the water's surface. Beware, too, of touching a stone when the fish is being brought into land. The touch of a stone or the bottom seems to spur a fish into another dash for freedom, and amongst stones this can result in a lost fish. Sometimes a very lightly hooked fish will make frenzied jumps and rushes. A tight line here can be equally disastrous, especially if the rod is at all stiff or allowed to exert too much pressure on the potentially weakest point of contact – the fish's mouth tissue.

The Effect of Salt Water on Tackle

AWAY from the river mouth, out in the bay and along the coast, there are sea trout waiting to be caught with fly or spinner, both fished in exactly the same way as one would on a loch – the wet fly cast, and the spinner cast, trolled or harled. The fly patterns may be different, but the same tackle can be used without ill effects to your rod or line, so long as the normal precautions are taken: washing the line, reel, rod and flies in fresh, preferably running, water after use to remove all traces of sea water. It is necessary to do this after fishing any sea pool or brackish water. In fact, with a strong breeze coming in from the sea enough unseen salt spray and moisture is swept upstream to have a detrimental effect on one's tackle, so keep this in mind if at all near the sea. It will take a little time, especially after a hard day's fishing when we may not feel like it, but it's only a five-minute job and there really is no alternative. A special kit for salt water would still require this care and attention and with present-day costs it would be rather a luxury.

In the sea

Scan the water for any sign of fish and if you see one jump, then there will be others. Your boat should be pulled along slowly while you cast a fairly long line with small flies and let the movement of the boat fish out the cast. Have a couple of feet of slack line, a belly in the line, to release as soon as a fish is hooked or takes one of the flies. To tighten before the fish has turned with the fly means a fish touched but not securely hooked – and with the soft mouth a lightly hooked fish is usually a lost fish, sooner if not later. Very great care has to be taken if all the fish risen in this way are not just to be pricked.

Tide, Tackle and Another Memory

When the rivers flowing into the sea are low and consequently the fish are not running, they move in and out with each tide. At low tide they tend to be far out. Thus the bays between headlands and the coastline itself have fish passing with each tide in each direction, in as well as out. I have often seen it so, and, as seems general in our mainland estuaries, they do take best at dusk and during the first few hours of the night, especially during the peak period of June and July. A drifting boat is best when there are plenty of fish on the move. There is little disturbance from a drifting boat and the fish are moving all the time – not in lies as in freshwater lochs.

A good breeze is best, and my most successful cast has been of three flies: Teal Blue and Silver, Grouse and Claret, Peter Ross (sizes 8 and 10) and, by way of variation, a Badger or Elverine Guineafowl Terror. Fishing three flies causes few problems since in boat fishing only a short line is cast – though a netted fish can make a mess of one's leader.

One of my first sea-fishing outings was many years ago

during a period of summer drought in the rivers. Fish were showing, making long V-shaped furrows on the surface. I was not quite certain what they were. I cast my flies over them – and soon there was no doubt about them being sea trout. And what a handful each one proved to be! They went mad when hooked and I took fish up to 3½lb but then I seemed to hook a much bigger one, which turned out to be three mackerel which had taken my three flies almost simultaneously.

Spinning can be very productive in the sea, and, in fact, whether or not there is a spate, trolling along the coast with a small Devon or a silver Mepps spoon can produce sea trout at any time from early June until the end of September.

5

SEA TROUT AT NIGHT

Loch Fishing

As darkness comes, fish are inclined to move into shallow bays, so if you are fishing during the day leave those alone if you can rather than disturb them. Fish the other end of the bay or even a part of the bay some distance away. Then when dusk comes you can start the drift over the shallow water, ideally not much more than four or five feet deep.

For dusk fishing, certainly to start with, use the same flies and ways of fishing them that you use during the day. A fish which has risen to take a natural fly will almost certainly take an artificial cast in front of it as soon as possible after you have seen the rise. Do not always retrieve the fly at once. Leave it there for a time to see what happens.

If you have seen a fish rise, head-and-tailing, you can be fairly certain that it is going to continue in that same direction after it has gone under. This time of the evening is frequently calm – though, had I the choice, I would prefer a light breeze to ruffle the water surface. In calm or comparatively calm conditions, very great care must be taken to avoid disturbance in the form of vibration waves from the boat.

Fish can easily be put down. Rocking the boat, even only once, sends out shock waves. Any knocks on the boat with an oar, a pipe being tapped out, a studded boot thumping against the floorboards can produce vibrations which will reach the fish and alarm them. It is all too easy to rock the boat without even being aware of it, and here is a real problem for the user of a short rod. With a short rod it is difficult to cast the longish line often required in fairly quiet and calm conditions without any body movement. This movement sends out waves from the boat and effectively forms a dead area reaching from the boat to the flies and perhaps beyond them.

Poor results under these fairly calm conditions can usually be traced back to vibration. Sea trout are very easily disturbed and this must never be forgotten. I have been in the middle of a shoal of rising char only to give the boat one gentle rock and see the area become instantaneously dead, with the nearest rise well out of casting range. Sea trout react in exactly the same way.

One effective way of overcoming vibration is to have the boat pulled gently, quietly and slowly along while you cast a fairly long line a few degrees forward of the boat's motion and to let the movement of the boat fish the flies through. They will move quickly enough without the rod being raised or the line recovered by hand. It is not necessary to strike at a rise, and, indeed, if the boat is moving at a reasonable rowing speed, a foot or two of line should be given to the fish at the rise.

Having two people in a boat doubles the danger of sending out shock waves. I much prefer to be alone in these calm conditions and just give the boat a couple of strokes on the oars at a time, letting it glide along between strokes as I fish out to the side.

How Many Flies?

As dusk falls it is not necessary to fish a bob fly, but when the technique of fishing it in the daylight has been mastered, it is not easy to give it up as it does raise and catch fish right on into the darkness. It is not difficult to fish the bob on the surface even during the darkest of nights. However, three flies can become a nuisance if not a downright hazard when a fish is caught and netted at night. The tangle of cast and net can be almost permanent, but thankfully things are not always like that. It is a matter of personal preference whether one, two or three flies are used. If it is calm or there is only a slight breeze, I use nylon of 6lb breaking strain with size 8 flies. If the breeze is nice and not too strong, 8lb nylon – but always three flies. I fish with the fullest confidence only when I have complete faith in my tackle. It is the only way to get the best results and derive the fullest enjoyment from one's fishing.

It is not always necessary to have a perfectly balanced outfit of rod, reel and line. Ill-balanced tackle can yield a great deal of satisfaction to augment the degree of enjoyment in fishing. An essential in this is that the line should not be light but, rather, too heavy for the rod. The long rod has an added advantage in the dark in that the actual casting is a slower movement than with a short rod and the danger of getting tangles and so-called wind knots is reduced. The flies I like for a pleasant light breeze to almost flat calm conditions are good on most lochs, but, as always, some may have a best killer not included in my few. Still, in general, I would be happy anywhere with a Watson's Fancy, a Cinnamon and Gold, a Coachman, a Black Pennell and a Peter Ross.

Larger Flies

THE sea trout does not always rise to the smaller flies and often a salmon fly of size 1 or 1/0 will kill them when it is dark or almost dark. The big fly is fished singly on 8lb breaking strain nylon. Be careful to use well tried knots.

Whatever casts and flies are being used, the flies must be fished slowly – very slowly. True enough, fish are caught with fast-moving flies sometimes, but, as I have stated elsewhere, sea trout can be unpredictable, particularly fresh and running fish, and they may be caught in the strangest of ways. The settled fish is not so fickle and the determination to fish for it will bring the others as an extra to the basket. I almost said 'by-product', but that would have been unkind to this great fish.

It is wise to have a large net in the boat and a torch. Use the torch as little as possible and always shaded and kept from shining either directly or indirectly on the water. A lighted cigarette or blazing match should also be shaded from the water. Petty and unnecessary, you may say. Well, so have it – but the fish won't.

The Take

THE take of a fish is invariably as though weed were being hooked – a sluggish drag, difficult to detect with the heavy line, but easy with a light line and sensitive rod, which will transmit such delicate messages from fly to hand even with twenty-five yards between. It is strange and I don't think it is imagination, but it does seem to be the pattern that a fish can be landed more quickly in the dark than during daylight hours.

I remember one evening when I had taken a surgeon friend out on a loch. He had just had his last day's fishing of the year and it had been a disappointing one. Although I did not know it then, it was the last fishing he was ever to do. There was only a slight breeze in the early dusk and I pulled the boat along slowly for him to cast to the side. He rose a lovely sea trout, played it beautifully, but, alas, as he drew it quietly in on its side to the net without a semblance of a jerk or slackening the hook came away from its hold, to go 'flip' behind his head. For a moment the fish lay mesmerised at its release just out of net range before it slowly rolled back onto an even keel and then went down into the depths. What a sickening feeling for us both, but my sorrow was more for him than for the loss of the fish. There were to be no more rises until darkness fell.

As I continued to draw the boat along slowly in the dark, my friend, who was using my rod and a cast with three flies on it, began to get pulls from 'weeds' on every other cast. At least, it seemed to him that the pulls were from weeds. I just could not get him to hook these weeds either by varying his response to the pull or by my own manipulation of the boat. He was finding it increasingly difficult to cast and fish correctly because of his frustration, so he gave me the rod. I had one or two casts and hooked the 'weeds' well and truly.

The hooking was not a strike, nor a giving of line, but merely a momentary easing of my hand and rod as I pictured the fish completing its turn. To strike at once was too soon, and to give it line would have been too late. How very narrow the margin between success and failure can be in a loch in pitch darkness. Generally the tendency is to be too slow with the strike and because of that I advise striking

77

quickly. My friend played the fish until it was almost ready for netting, but now he was at a loss, not being able to see anything and not knowing what to do. It takes a little experience to bring in a fish in total darkness, but it is not difficult to judge its position and to bring it into a net one is holding oneself. We had not seen it, but I knew that it was a very big fish.

My friend wanted to net it himself and he produced a small pencil torch – which, no doubt, he used for gazing at tonsils or perhaps retinae. He shone it into the water and sure enough a huge eye stared back at him out of the darkness. We knew then what Cyclops must have looked like. The shock passed and the fish was netted – a lovely sea trout of 13½lb. By then it was getting late so we headed for home. It was to be the last of many great nights I had there.

Forty-five years later it is all too evident that the number of fish in that loch now is comparatively small. The explanation for this remains in the realm of conjecture, but widespread UDN, the loss of spawning areas and excessive netting at sea as well as in the estuaries must bear much of the responsibility. The taking of kelts must also be a contributory factor. I am confident that stocks will recover from the effects of UDN and time is bringing a more enlightened approach to the other problems. I remember from previous days how extensive poaching was at spawning time – both for the ova as well as for fish for salting – but I also remember from the 1920s the unfounded fears for future stocks.

Boat and Bank

In many ways and for many reasons it is better to fish from a boat. All the water can be fished, rising fish can be reached and, perhaps most important of all in many places, the flies are being drawn from the shallow water into the deep. Bank fishing, however, has its advantages. You avoid the disturbance caused when a boat is rocked or perhaps knocked, which often happens when a fish is hooked. Sea trout do move around at night and when fishing from the bank it is not necessary to move much from place to place. Wading must be done carefully. Waves sent out when wading disturb the water being fished. It is strange, I admit, but it does seem true that while sea trout can jump and splash as they will without apparently disturbing the other fish in the vicinity a careless step when wading will put them down.

The whir of a sea trout when it jumps is a wonderful sound at night. Cast a long line and let it settle a few moments before drawing it in very slowly. Again, the take is exactly like hooking weed and, unfortunately, this does happen at times. A large fly can be fished very effectively from the bank, but really only when large sea trout can be reasonably expected. I know of a number of places where a salmon outfit is used and there is no real reason why it shouldn't be – the fish are like salmon in size. If there is a shingle shore or clean bank it is often easy to tail the sea trout caught, and it has to be very dark before it is too dark for this. Tailing avoids the risk of the cast becoming entangled in the net.

Problems of Moonlight

THE moon produces brightness as well as shadow, both of which can be as disturbing as the brightest of sunshine, yet I have caught many sea trout as well as the odd salmon in the moonlight and risen a great many of both. It does not mean defeat for me, but for some strange reason nowadays it does not present a challenge I feel prepared to take up. This may be because I have already had too many dark nights for more to tempt me out, though it was not always the case.

For a number of years this moonlight glare had me

completely beaten. There were plenty of rises but few captures, and then, one night in a cloudless sky, it suddenly occurred to me that the glint of the cast and the rod as well as other shadows were causing the short rises, just as happens in sunlight when drifting down with the sun behind you. I put on a cast of smaller flies, size 10, on a 2x gut cast (today's equivalent is 4lb breaking strain) and started to fish into the moonlight. It was also into the wind but, with the boat being pulled along slowly so that I was fishing over good water, success came immediately and a good basket resulted. Remembering this prevented failure on many subsequent occasions.

When occasional clouds shade the moon try to fish the best lies during the periods of shade. Sea trout take well in them. It is not only cloud that provides shade. Good fishing can continue in shadowy places after the moon has risen and spoiled most of the fishing – as it will unless there is a good breeze. A rocky point, the shoulder of a hill or the proximity of trees may give decreasing shade long after the moon has risen.

The River at Night

IN the river, sea trout start to rise freely at dusk and continue to do so well after dark. Most of them slip back to the tail of the pool or into the shallows. Whether it is true or imagined that the fish does not play as well at night does not really matter, because a sea trout is a handful at any time and perhaps a settled fish more so than a tired fresh-run one.

A walk by the river in daytime is really essential if no satisfactory advice is available and is in any case a wise plan in order to check the latest details of fish, snags, trees, places for landing fish, and so on before venturing out into the dark, when every obstacle seems twice as large, deep and difficult.

On one occasion on the Driva river in Norway I had some fine night fishing for sea trout – until a number of fellow anglers of sundry nationalities heard of my success. Their idea was a real hunting expedition. Fires were lit and blazed merrily on the shingle banks; rods of all types were stacked like rifles in Wild West style; Toby spinners flew in all directions. Few fish were seen after this and I moved on to the quieter waters for success. Perhaps this careless approach and low standard of fishing contributes to poorer catches – certainly, the waters and stocks of fish are not entirely to blame.

Wading

WADE only when it is absolutely essential, whether in loch or river, by day or by night. Do wade carefully. I am talking about safety or comfort – you must look to yourself in that respect. Careless wading sends out waves over both loch and pool which stop fish rising for a time if not for the remainder of the evening or night. The fish seem to know when the waves come from a source of possible danger. Naturally this does not apply when there is a good breeze, but it does when there is a soft, light breeze, which is the best of all, and, of course, in the dead calm when the fish take well if fine tackle is used.

Lights

THE light of a cigarette, match or torch must be shaded from the water more carefully than when fishing a loch. I know of the luminous lures used for night fishing but I believe firmly that sea trout can see as well if not better in the dark than they can in daylight. On a black night their eyesight is very acute. It is interesting to note that not so long ago a team of zoologists more or less proved by experiment that fish are not colour-blind and that they have not only their likes but also their dislikes in colour.

Tackle for the River

THE long rod is ideal for night work. It makes it easy to keep the line clear of the bank, bushes, trees, and snags in the river which cause many difficulties for the user of the short rod. I use a fine line for night fishing because of the ultrasensitivity it offers between fly and hand, which gives a feeling of contact with the fly at all times and the knowledge that the fly is doing what you want it to do. This feeling and knowledge is very important with all fishing, whether for early spring salmon or the more exciting sea trout at night.

Resist the temptation to use heavy tackle, though the cover of darkness may tempt you to. A fine cast is as important at night as it is during the day, but in stormy conditions a large fly can be used just as on the loch. I have demonstrated so often that the difference between a leader of 7lb breaking strain and one of 6lb can be the difference between failure and success in late dusk or dark. With 7lb nylon rises from fish resulted in just a touch or even a short tug but no real contact. I have fished with it on purpose with the intention of landing a big fish a little quicker than I could with the 6lb cast. It has always been the same – only touches from the rises until I have switched to 6lb nylon, when all are good takes. My own choice is a cast of three flies, and I have yet to find a better team for night fishing than a Watson's Fancy on the top dropper, a Cinnamon and Gold on the middle, and a Coachman on the tail. On occasions other flies have also done well, but these three along with the Peter Ross, the Jungle Cock and Gold and the Kate McLaren are usually found in my lapel.

Fankles are easy to come by when a fish is hooked and landed and it is a prudent angler who has some spare made-up casts with him, ready for use. If you don't like fishing three flies, a tapered cast with only one fly does well and there are none of the dangers inherent in using three, when the two flies not in the fish can catch in weeds, snags or the net, or in your hand as you tail a fish. A single fly greatly reduces the bird's-nest potential in the dark.

Midge Repellents

A THOUGHT about midges. There are many excellent repellents, but do be careful not to let any repellent get on your cast or flies. I have no proof, only a strong suspicion, that if any of the repellent does get on either the cast or the flies it frightens the fish, or at least makes them warier. Friends who take a fishing annually and extend an open invitation to my wife and me to fish with them have some good but perhaps limited sea trout fishing at night for a few nights in June, when a number of large fish are in the pools and may be caught – having come up in the April run, they are quite dark coloured. My friends are excellent anglers, but the midges do bother them, and they have no choice but to use a repellent, some of which, I'm afraid, does get on their casts. They take care, certainly, but a rub of a hand on a face, a touch of the cast, and the damage is done. Often, too often, we caught good baskets whilst they had only a few fish, and our standards are about equal. We did not use any repellents. Recently my friends have tried to manage without repellents and their catches have increased. These lovely June evenings, when it never really becomes dusk in the north of Britain, give a perfect setting for fishing. The warmth and the stillness is broken only by the chirp of a woodcock overhead or by the drumming of a snipe.

Fishing Sidelights

How true it is that it is not all of fishing to fish. So many decry night fishing, often necessary for sea trout, but they do so just because they do not know the joys of it. I have met a deer on the path in the trees by the river in almost complete darkness and thought I would die on the spot. It may be that rigor mortis, or at least something very like it, can set in before death! I don't know how the deer felt.

Fishing gives us so many memories, apart from those of catching fish. Another incident which comes to mind was when I was fishing a small, black pool in the dark, I could reach the whole of it from one spot on the grass which extended down to the pool from the bank about twenty yards behind. I had caught two fish of about two pounds or so and laid them on the grass, well back from the river. Another fish came my way and when I had put it where I thought the others were the darkness put doubt in my mind as to whether they really were there or a little farther along the bank. I killed a fourth fish, but could only find my third one. I thought of cats and rats, but the culprit I caught with one of the fish was a hedgehog. The other fish had completely vanished and I don't know what happened to them. The hedgehog kept his fish and I took two home. I must confess that I still leave my fish lying around when I catch them, but it is really not wise.

Notable Nights

My first wife and I did not get out fishing much together although nothing gave me greater pleasure, but I remember we had some fine fishing during four evenings one week. We had 29 sea trout weighing a total of 76½lb. The three heaviest fish were 10½, 10 and 9½lb, plus five salmon, total weight 48lb. My wife had most of them, possibly because she fished more, but it may not have been entirely so, since she fished well. As usual I got the biggest.

Tackle

HE who is not a true expert with the small rod just cannot succeed with it. The take of the sea trout in the dark can be a remote and faraway light drag, rather like the feel of a puff of wind on the rod. Recognising it is difficult and, I would say, beyond the sensitivity of many. The tackle I use makes it as easy as it can be made with any tackle I have seen and handled. It isn't that I cannot cast a line with the short rod – I can. The light line and long rod are ill-balanced in the eyes of fishing tackle salesmen and the expert, but only because the length of line normally recommended to be cast with the rod is so much shorter than the length of fine line required to give the correct weight of line outside the rod point. A little more power in casting may be needed and the pause for the line to straighten out behind is longer than normal, but it is not difficult and the fine line will cast into the wind quite well. Unfortunately, there is little margin for error in the timing and execution of the cast. If incorrectly executed, the cast with a light line is, in all senses and without a doubt, a flop.

BAIT FISHING AND SPINNING

BOTH bait fishing and spinning can provide good sport, but
they are not permitted on many waters. I have had some
great fun and good baskets of sea trout with worm and
spinner and some good evenings with the natural elver, but
even so I much prefer fly fishing. That is one reason why this
chapter will be short. Another reason is that a reduction in
the amount of bait fishing and spinning in waters which are
good for fly will make more good fly fishing available to

everyone. There is no doubt that, on the whole, spinning and bait fishing harm fly fishing – and not only for sea trout.

Tackle for Worming

WHEN worming I use the same rod and light line that I use for fly fishing, whether the water is high and dirty or low and clear. My reason is basically the same as it is for fly fishing. It is that I am in contact with the bait all the time. I know what it is doing and I can feel the lead bumping over the stones as well as the faintest stop of a take. The long rod gives greater range, more water is fished and snags are more easily avoided. The worm can be cast easily without being flicked off and it doesn't get dragged downstream as quickly as when a heavy line is used. When rivers are low, the white water and little corners so much favoured by sea trout can be fished from afar with little risk of disturbing the fish.

The nylon leader should be nine feet or so in length. This allows fishing without the line being in the water at all times. A few lead shot are needed on the cast. The actual amount depends on the force of the stream being fished, but even in still water one or two are needed. The shot should be between eighteen inches and two feet from the hook. Many prefer the two-hook Pennell or the three-hook Stewart tackle, but I like the Stewart tackle in low water only and the Pennell not at all.

Types of Worm

THERE are many varieties of worms. I prefer to have plenty of all sizes of the black-headed worm. They should be kept in dry moss and oatmeal for a few days in the old-fashioned way, for the purpose of toughening them up. I have no doubt that there are other ways of toughening them up. The red worms do not seem to toughen so well, nor do they appear to be as attractive to sea trout as the dusky ones, and the white worm seems useless.

Where to Fish

THE sea trout does not take the worm well in slack water, but it will take it in streams where it will sometimes not look at a fly during the day. Pools of rushing white water are favourite places. On occasions a heavy sinker is required, but there is no need to use the heavy tackle, so often the outfit of many fishing in dirty water or white water below a fall. Not all falls cause fish to congregate in the pools below them, only those which present some obstacle, such as the fall being too high for them to jump, or the river being too high with too great a volume of water coming over during full flood or part flood. Worm fishing ranges from a crude style, which may be all that is necessary in highly coloured water, to a style demanding a very high degree of skill to produce results in clear water, whether in river or estuary. Approach the stream or place to be fished with great care. Keep out of sight. Whenever possible, cast the worm up-stream and fish it down, bumping on the bottom of the river and, as it goes downstream of you, let out line so that it can continue on its way a few yards and slowly move in towards the side. At all times during its journey down, keep in distinct contact with the bait. Have a few feet of slack line in your hand to give to the fish as it turns away and moves off with the worm before you strike.

There may be many sea trout in pools and the streams of rivers in low water which seldom take the fly during the day but which provide good sport at night. It is as well to remember that worming and spinning these areas during the day does great damage to the night fishing. Sea trout do not recover from the disturbance readily and even fresh-run fish move on quickly. The comparatively stale fish is usually a very careful fellow. Night fishing gives by far the greater yield of fish, though many anglers may not like the hazards of night fishing and are content with a little sport in comparative comfort during daylight hours.

Tackle for Spinning

THERE is no shortage of information about spinning rods and reels and there are innumerable varieties of both. I like a short supple rod of 7 feet or so and a fixed-spool reel with the full bale pick-up. It is comforting to have two spools full of nylon, one on the reel and the other spare. One spool carries 8lb breaking strain and one with 10lb – the fine nylon to be used with the finer tackle and the heavy to be used in spates and fast, rough water. In this way you avoid much of the frustration caused by repeated breaks when you try to cast a fairly heavy weight on thin nylon, and the annoyance trying to cast a light weight against the drag of heavy nylon. Casting is much easier and indeed is only really successful with a full spool of nylon. When the spool is, say, only half-full, there is a considerable braking effect as the nylon comes off the spool and rubs against the rim. This greatly reduces distance.

Nylon stretches. Take care not to wind it onto the spool of your reel under too much tension. The pressure caused by the elasticity of the nylon can crack the spool. The length of nylon between the tip of the rod and the weight is usually the same at each cast and this throws extra strain on the nylon at the rod tip. It pays to keep a constant check that there is no weakening at this point. Nylon is cheap and fish are beyond price from the sporting point of view, so cut off and destroy doubtful sections of nylon.

Spinning Baits

MY favourite spinners are blue and silver Devons in sizes from one to two inches in length. I also like to have some which spin clockwise and others that spin anticlockwise, and I use them alternately in order to prevent any serious kinking in the line. The Mepps spoon is also one of my favourites. I think that the Devon attracts fish which the Mepps would not otherwise even interest, but the Devon doesn't hook them quite so well as the Mepps. The Mepps spoon is easier to fish in comparatively shallow water. I have already referred to spools of nylon of 8 and 10lb BS, but very much finer nylon is required with a small light bait which must be used under very clear and difficult conditions.

There are many spinning baits and wobbling baits on the market. Basically they fall into two categories – the spoons and the plugs. Even the spoons fall into two types. Some wobble through the water, such as the Toby and the Tilly, or, for that matter, the ordinary spoon which you can hammer out yourself in a few minutes. Others whirl, of which the Mepps is the best-known example. I favour a fly spoon greatly and this is a little whirling spoon like a small Mepps. I cast it with my salmon fly rod and fish it much as I would a fly and it has killed many a good fish in heavy water. I have no fixed views on plug baits, although some that I have seen would, no doubt, prove tremendously effective. For instance, there is the Rapala, a splendid wobbling bait which already has a good reputation on many waters for both salmon and sea trout.

Basic Principles

THE main principles to bear in mind when spinning for sea trout in rivers is that the bait must be given a lively motion. Very often sea trout will respond only to a bait which is moving fast across their lies. It is the opposite with salmon, which very often move only to a bait which is in or over their lies. In lochs there is no fixed rule, as the bait may be moved quickly or slowly under differing conditions. The quickly moving bait in a loch is fishing at a shallow level and the slowly moving one fishes deeper. Experimenting with speeds and depths in order to determine the temperament of the fish on the day will be of invaluable help in achieving a good basket.

Spinning Techniques

As with salmon, wherever possible draw the bait into deeper water and not into the shallows or onto rocks. If this principle is followed in river fishing you will find fewer fish turning away from the spinner at the last moment. The problem of fish turning away will, however, be encountered from time to time. One very good technique for taking these fish is to speed up the bait towards the end of the retrieve. Occasionally, a deft cast beyond a retreating fish which has previously missed the bait will induce it to take it cleanly.

Sea Trout and the Spinner

A STALE sea trout does not usually fall for the spinner. It takes it very seldom in the loch and seldom in a river, unless it has moved up the river recently. A clean-run sea trout takes it readily in both loch and river.

Many fish touch the Devon without being hooked. Perhaps the set-up of the Devon contributes to this. The small single triangle just behind the metal body is not the best of hooking devices and a small triangle on the shoulder of the minnow might improve its hooking powers. The old type of minnow with slots in the side two trebles may have lost its popularity because of its readiness to become hooked up on weeds or snags.

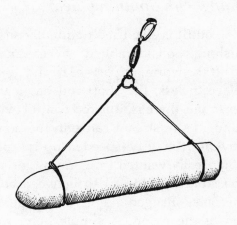

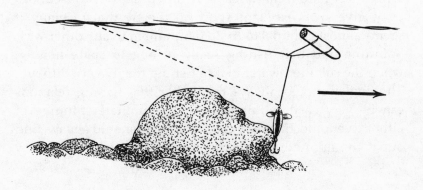

Line Releaser

Worming with Spinning Gear

THE spinning outfit is also used frequently and successfully for worm fishing. Considerable distances can be cast without flicking off the worm, or parts of it, and great accuracy is attained. Nevertheless, the short rod has many disadvantages. For example, there is little rod control over the bait. Its swings round in the stream can only be adjusted by the release of nylon. It may be speeded up by rod movement, but this is not really wanted in worming for sea trout. It is almost impossible to guide a bait between boulders and if the tackle becomes snagged there is the danger of straining a long section of the nylon. A simple home-made wooden releaser is an invaluable gadget to have in one's bag. If you should snag up, avoid winding the reel against the clutch without recovering line – it kinks the nylon.

The celluloid anti-kink vane is, I find, better than the usual type of swivel at the link between the main nylon and the cast. It is light, unobtrusive and highly effective. I use tucked half blood-knots to attach swivels and baits.

In conclusion, let me stress that spinning and bait fishing for sea trout are techniques. A bait is used, not abused. Sea trout give such excellent sport on the fly that to many it seems almost criminal to try to tempt them in any other way. Spinning and bait fishing really belong to spate fishing, when the coloured water makes fishing the fly very difficult. The angler should always remember that fishing relations can be very easily strained by indiscriminate spinning of either river or loch. In any case, an angler should always find out if the minnow is permitted before he fishes it on any water.

—7—

Dapping

The Origins

I DON'T know who introduced dapping to Loch Maree, nor does it really matter, but I can well remember in the late 1920s that one of my tasks used to be catching live daddy-long-legs for anglers. I put them into a cardboard box about four inches square. In the lid of the box there was a small flap, two inches long and one inch wide. This flap could be lifted and one or two daddy-long-legs taken out and impaled on the hook. It was not a very good container, but it served its purpose.

Live daddy-long-legs had a wonderful attraction for sea trout both on as well as off the hook, for many escaped to become the sea trouts' prey before they could be put on the hook. Whilst this meant good feeding for the sea trout and perhaps made them a little careless at the sight of a nice, juicy long-legged tasty bite, the difficulty in catching crane-flies in sufficiently large numbers and getting them out of the box and on the hook without losing too many was so great that the artificial dapping fly was most welcome when it arrived. It was not at all unusual for all the daddy-long-legs to escape, producing a wonderful rise of sea trout, with not a single live fly left to fish with – a near tragic situation.

Dapping can be great fun and it can provide much of the sport and joy of fishing for a larger number of people than could ever experience it by other methods. It is not difficult to dap and catch fish. For the beginner it is much easier, in my experience, than the wet or the dry fly. It is easier to become an expert with the blow line than with the wet fly outfit, but the difficulties of striking are real and almost as great as for the wet fly, and I shall consider this elsewhere.

Advantages of the Dap

SEA trout tend to be slow to rise and they are particularly slow to do so when lying in deep water. This is one of the reasons why the dap is so effective and is so popular. The dapped fly is on the water all the time and is moving comparatively slowly in about the same area of water whereas the wet fly is often moving faster through the water so that it is past and gone before the trout can rise. The dapped fly therefore gives the trout more time to see it and to rise.

It is not easy to keep a wet fly fishing as slowly as the dap which will give the trout a chance to come up. It can be done, however, once you have the technique, and then the wet fly can be more effective than the dap. Using three wet flies, the top dropper produces the same effects as the dapped fly and in addition you have the benefits that come from fishing the middle dropper and the tail fly as well.

There is no denying the fact that dapping does not require as much skill as wet fly fishing, but why be frustrated by three unruly wet flies when the wind will blow out your dap and have you fishing well without all the bother of casting? The person who prefers to dap gets as much pleasure and satisfaction out of it as I do out of my style of fishing, and that is as it should be. One can be taught to dap in a few minutes; not so with casting. Dapping does have its limitations, and without a good breeze it is but memory. The limpness of floss in a dead calm is no joy to behold and it can be extremely frustrating in a very light breeze.

Popularity

As the years have passed, so dapping has become more and more popular. Most of the anglers who dap do so efficiently and confidently and it is the only method of fishing used by many – with the result that very much more water is fished effectively than ever before. This gives the impression that more fish are caught by dapping than by the wet fly because it is the more effective method of fishing for sea trout on a loch. In my experience, it is not just that. Because in the right conditions dapping is the easier method, it is effective in the hands of a vast number who would only succeed with the wet fly in proportion to their degree of luck.

Missed Fish

I HAVE heard it said that more fish are missed and pricked and frightened or disturbed by the dap than by the wet fly,

but I cannot agree. A fish risen to the dap can usually be seen, whereas many rises and touches to the wet fly may never be seen or felt, although pricked sufficiently to disturb them. In my opinion, there are more rises to a team of wet flies than there are to the dap.

Dapping Flies

THE natural daddy-long-legs has been replaced by many artificial flies in a great variety of colours, but I tend to stick to a Black Pennell, a Bucktail, a Red Palmer or a Loch Ordie. There are, of course, specially dressed flies for dapping, usually on single hooks, sometimes with a small treble tied in at the shoulder or extending at the rear as a flying treble. An application of some good floatant is required, otherwise the fly becomes waterlogged and unfishable. When a fish is caught the fly usually gets bedraggled and must be replaced, so have a few spare ones ready for use. When the breeze is strong, a large fly is needed, and for a lighter breeze, a lighter fly, but, strangely enough, a small fly of size 8 is not effective, although it is an excellent size of wet fly for use as a top dropper. Sometimes two dapping flies are used at the one time, but I do not like this. One fly is very much easier to fish, and because of this it is probably fished better.

The Dapping Rod

IN order to get the dapping fly fishing out in front of us in the breeze we need a long rod. One of fourteen feet is ideal. It has to be held in more or less the same position all the time so it must be light. The modern telescopic dapping rods are very convenient.

The Line

THE silk or nylon floss line should be broad enough to offer maximum surface to the wind and sail on easily, taking the fly forward under the angler's guidance. Fine, light nylon floss does not puff out so well in light winds, though it has the advantage in strong winds. It is quite satisfactory to attach a length of floss to your fly line – fourteen feet or so is all that is required – but it is better to have a full twenty yards of floss spliced to plenty of backing on any suitable reel. The fly can be tied directly to the floss but I prefer a couple of feet of 7 or 8lb nylon, usually strong enough for any fish. After all, a fish is to be played, not hoisted in.

8

HOOKING AND PLAYING

BEFORE a fish can be played it must be hooked, which means
that enough pressure must be applied to put the hook over
the barb into some part of the fish's mouth. The application
of this pressure may be in the form of a definite strike or
merely a tightening of the line, depending on the type of the
rise and the size of the hook used. The influence of the latter
is simple. The larger the fly, the greater the force necessary to
put it home.

Rises

RISES are of an infinite variety and range from an unseen pull from a fish to a splash in a fast stream; from the slow head-and-tail rise of a fish to the kind of rise when a fish jumps completely out of the water and onto the fly.

When the line straightens slightly on a loch and the breeze is fair with the boat drifting well, an immediate strike is needed. The fish has almost certainly got the fly in its mouth and is moving towards you with it or turning away. On occasions it might be right to delay for a second, but there are so many more fish which take in this way and are missed because of a late strike rather than one too soon that it is wise to strike immediately. There is no guide or way of judging each take.

Occasionally a fish is on before you know what has happened. A flash, a splash, a tug, and that's it. The fish is hooked. The question of whether to strike or not doesn't arise. However, if you are an advocate of striking (as I am), do not give it a second strike just to make sure that it is well hooked. To my mind this is really asking for trouble.

Striking

THE actual strike is not the violent or frantic strike so many anglers make by a reflex action when the rod is brought back with a jerk. That only serves to break rods, leaders and even human hearts. All that is required is a firm and properly timed tightening on the fish. The degree varies with the type of tackle used and with the speed of the water in which the fish has risen. A raising of the rod point by wrist action is all that is required.

If a fish takes when the rod is pointing straight downstream or at the fish and the line and cast are more or less in a straight line from the reel to the fly, or if only a very short line is out, it is necessary to give line in the strike and perhaps to move the rod point towards the fish as well, to give it the freedom to turn with the fly. Only when the fish has turned away or continued down with the fly can the strike be made – if, indeed, the tightening can be called a strike.

Delay in Striking

THE ability to wait before striking as well as the patience to do so is put to the full test if a fairly long line is being fished and the fish jumps clean out of the water, taking the fly when it comes down into the water again. Sometimes a fly is taken on the way out and it must be let go with the fish and not held. The use of Polaroid glasses so often calls for the exercise of great restraint when one has a rise. The fish may then be seen coming to the fly when it is still a long way from it. Many fish are risen and missed in water being fished from a stance high above it and this is because the fish is seen so soon. The slightest movement of the rod point pulls the fly away.

Other Rise Forms

A FISH which produces only a boil on the surface should be struck at the sight of the boil. Those which rise head and tail, in any direction, should not be struck until the tail is disappearing. Some rise towards you and you must handle them quickly to keep the strain on as it comes in. Sometimes you have to stand up to avoid bringing the rod too far back. A rise may come very close to the boat and then very great care is needed. The rod may be upright, with the line coming down to the water at an acute angle to the point of the rod. A strike from this position is a very chancy affair.

Whatever the type of rise, picture it as it occurs. Picture

the movement of the fish, and strike when it has turned away with the fly. A boil rise, for example, is seen after the fish has turned away with or without the fly. A head-and-tail rise is a delight to see and so easy to strike perfectly – yet it requires so much self-restraint. Seeing a head-and-tail rise and striking it correctly is my greatest joy in fishing. If a fish misses the fly, do not strike at all, however tempting the prospect. Draw the flies on – the fish may well rise again during the same cast. This also avoids the risk that the fish might be disturbed by the sudden departure of the flies.

Missed Fish

REFERENCES to fish 'missing the fly' may or may not be very accurate, but each may form his opinion about this when thinking of the oft-repeated story of the gentleman fishing the river, rising a salmon, but not hooking it. The ghillie said to him, 'You missed him!' A second cast was made over the fish, which rose again slowly, a lovely head-and-tail of a rise. Again no contact between the fish and the gentleman. The ghillie's remark: 'Dash! Missed again!' The third time the fish rose a few casts later and yet again no contact was made with the fish. Rather sharply, the ghillie said, 'Missed it again, Sir!' The fisherman was rather irritated by this and, turning to the ghillie, said, 'You have a go if you think you can do any better!' The ghillie did. At the second cast the fish rose and turned away, but wasn't hooked. The ghillie said, 'He missed it! Dash it!'

I think that all rising fish may well intend to take the fly, even though a fish may seem to keep its mouth firmly shut throughout the rise. The fact that the fish has risen to the fly shows that it was interested, but the slim interest has been destroyed by some weakness in our presentation – whether it is the thickness of the nylon, the size of the fly, its dressing, the speed of its movement, or one of many things we may do to disturb the fish.

Hooking Technique

I LIKE a free-running reel and I trap the line between my index finger and the cork handle, except when discretion or the fear of burning my finger with the line as it sizzles out makes me keep my finger well clear of it. For me, as for many others, it is the only way to assess the power of the strike and the pressure or strain at that very important moment after the fish is first hooked, as well as at other times too. The line can be released quickly – as it must when, for example, the rod is pointing straight at the fish or you are casting to the side while the boat is being rowed along between drifts, as well as in the other instances mentioned elsewhere. Then handlining is a great comfort, because you can hold the strain by the pressure of the finger on the line against the cork as slack line is wound onto the reel. Many experts handline by coiling the recovered line on their fingers and do not have any problem in getting rid of it to the fish or onto the reel. To the comparative novice this is an extremely difficult operation.

I prefer striking from the finger to striking from the reel for a number of reasons. There is no difficulty in setting the reel to the desired tension – the adjustments can be very fine and simple to make. The dangers arise from the inflexible nature of this tension. It can only be applied as set. Adjustment while playing a fish is rather fiddling and finicky. If your hands are in any way cold, it can be rather dangerous to attempt any alteration in the tension. In making the actual strike, a lightly set reel may scream out and inconveniently allow the point of the rod to go behind your head whilst retaining the strain. If the reel is set to prevent this happening, then it may also be too tight to allow the fish to make its first wild rush. Furthermore, the rod and line may not be in such a position as to bend from the minimum amount of strain from the reel.

A series of pictures comes to my mind with, at their centre, an angler who does not keep a finger on the line. A fish has risen as the left hand pulls in line. When it is hooked and comes towards the angler, if the left hand cannot retrieve any more line to keep the strain it is away back as far to the side as it can physically go. The hand dare not let go of the line and no more can be done in that area. It is difficult to get the line between the index finger and the cork without risking a fatal slackening of the line. The right hand holds the rod as high as possible, as well as being as far back as is feasible. The angler jumps to a standing position if in a boat, or steps back if on a bank. Do as he will, the fish may remain slack. Few fish carry co-operation far enough to allow this situation to become straightened out and resolved satisfactorily. Fish which are allowed slack line are not invariably lost, but it is wisest to consider them so.

Unfortunately, seeing the fish rise and then striking it correctly now concludes my joy in fishing. Playing it doesn't give me any real pleasure. I am always glad to have someone with me who will play the fish for me, whether a sea trout or a salmon, for my greatest pleasure now is watching the excitement of someone else playing and landing the fish.*

Playing a Fish

WHEN the fish has been risen and hooked, the rod must be kept well up and the line's tightness governed by many factors, of which two are the strength of the nylon and the likely softness or toughness of the fish's mouth. Whether or not the fish is lightly hooked can be estimated by reference to the type of rise, and speed of the current and, possibly, the behaviour of the fish itself.

* There are many anglers whose commitment to fishing stems from just that generous moment when Charles, having risen and hooked a fish, then handed the rod over for the playing. It was precisely in this manner that I first landed a salmon – T.G.L.

Any fish which has been up for some time plays harder than a fresh-run fish. This may be because a spell in the fresh water strengthens the toughness of the fins, or simply because the fish is more rested. But all of them can travel extremely fast from the moment of hooking, so you must be prepared for this. There must be no slack line lying around in such a way that it could catch on a coat button, round the butt of the rod or reel, around the reel handle or on floorboards or other snags such as burnt heather or twigs from bushes.

Losing Fish

A FISH may be lost for many reasons out of our control – but not always so. The risk of loss is greatly reduced if the rod is kept up so that its springiness keeps an even strain and doesn't make for a hard jerk which could either snap the nylon or tear out the hook. Lowering the rod increases the strain until maximum strain is reached when the rod is pointing straight at the fish. A steady pressure can be easily maintained if you control the line against the cork with your finger and do not overwind the reel or pull back the rod tip when the fish goes off in a mad rush.

One occasion when the rod must be lowered is when the fish makes a rush and then jumps. The rod point must be dropped in order to give line quickly to the fish as it speeds in the air with the drag of the line through the water holding it back. The strain at this moment is very great if the rod is held up and normal pressure applied. Very often the pull of the line is so heavy that the head of a leaping fish is held while its tail flies over and the cast is broken. As yet I do not have any explanation for other occasional losses. They can occur when the rod is handed to another person to play the fish or when you bring the top of the rod over your head to bring the fish round to the windward side of the boat.

Sulking Fish

In a loch a fish may sulk and be towed about for many hours. If there seems to be any danger of this happening, the surest way of speeding up the fight and ending it successfully is to go ashore in a weed-free area. This has never failed me in bringing about the fish's defeat.

The problem of sulking is more easily overcome in a river than in a loch. The water is generally shallower and it is usually possible to change the direction of the pull to get the fish to move. There tend to be many more snags in rivers than in lochs, though I know of some lochs which have an abundance of them, and the long rod is a great asset when bushes, rocks and shallows are encountered during the struggle. Not the least of its advantages is that it enables the angler to manoeuvre a fish up river on the far side of the current, which may be necessary if some obstruction prevents you going downstream and you have to land the fish at the neck of the pool. The fish can be guided up the far side of the stream and then swung across the stream into the comparative calm for either netting or tailing. It is not easy to pull it up the nearside against a stream when only light tackle and a short rod are being used.

Snags

In some pools the fish may go a long way off and into stones or other snags on the far shore. In a pool that you know it is usually possible to avoid snags by directing the fish elsewhere, but in a strange river it is just as well to assume that there are snags all along the far shore and to act accordingly and prudently, trying to direct the fish away from them.

Turning Fish

It is not always possible to prevent a fish which takes in slack, shallow water from leaving the pool. The current is often so slow that giving yards of line in order to exert a downstream pull on the fish does not work. (It is generally safe to assume that a fish will move in the opposite direction to the strain so long as it has the power to do so, though a tired fish may be carried downstream by its weight alone.)

There are many dangers when a fish leaves the pool in which it is hooked. The greatest is that the line may be taken round a boulder and snagged. This can be disastrous. Good switch casting is often successful in releasing it. On occasions the otter or releaser can be used to free the line, sometimes with the fish still on. When the fish has gone downstream it may be possible to clear a snag by letting the fish go a long way ahead and then lifting the line over the snag.

If snags are many, as when the river is low and the streams run between boulders, it is best to keep opposite the fish. This is equally important when the fish leaves the pool and moves upstream. Fortunately, this does not happen frequently, but it is very possible when a fish has been inadvertently foul-hooked, as can easily happen when three flies are being fished. Here the dangers are slightly different. The fish tends to swim deep in an upstream direction and, when it is tired, slip back, still pointing upstream, perhaps on the other side of a submerged rock. The current then holds the line against the rock and may jam it into a small crevice and cause a break before the angler can get upstream of it. Sometimes fish come back downstream head first at full pelt and unless you pick up the slack fast the line may get snagged. The slack is unlikely to be enough to enable the fish to slip the hook.

Landing Fish

WHEN a fish is being brought in for netting or tailing, it is sometimes easy to take a step or two backwards and continue to draw the fish in. This is better than reeling in:

vibration from the reel alarms the sea trout, particularly when the line is short, making it rush off again. In any case, if the fish is being brought in for tailing it finds renewed energy as soon as its belly touches the shore, and out it dashes again. One must be prepared for this and not try to hold the fish. Remember, the hold of the hook in the fish may be weakening and the strength of the nylon failing after the strain of the fight. Stepping back in this way keeps the fish from sulking.

When the fish is played out and ready for netting there are no further problems to be encountered if a large net is at hand – and it always should be in a boat on a good sea trout loch. If it is not, it is safest to beach the boat in a weed-free part of the loch and tail the fish on the shore. It is not wise to try to net a fish with a net which is patently too small for the job. I recall a friend trying to put an 11lb fish of mine into a net which would have been stretched to its limit with a 4lb fish. He did manage to get the fish on the bank and into the safe region very well, but it was standing on its head in the net with about two-thirds of its length in a graceful, but perhaps not delightful, curve above it.

Tailing and Gaffing

THE alternatives to a net are the tailer, the gaff and hand-tailing. The tailer is good but not for the smaller fish of 3 or 4lb, so a net may also have to be carried. As regards the gaff, I have noted with interest over the years the number of anglers, some of wide experience, who, when they go fishing for big fish – be it salmon, sea trout, or, indeed, brown trout – simply must carry a gaff. I have little use for one.

I hope that a few words on tailing fish will prove helpful to those who find themselves in the delightful position of having hooked a fish too large for their net. It is not at all

Tailing a sea trout

Taking hold of a large sea trout

essential to carry a huge net or gaff when fishing from the bank. I agree that there are times when a gaff might be useful, but I disagree with the indiscriminate gaffing of every sizeable fish, irrespective of the conditions. The mere fact of carrying a gaff can lead to this, and it is also extra weight to be carried.

I seldom use a gaff and never like using one, however necessary it may seem. There are few places in all the waters I know where I could not land a fish without one. In any case, it is a rather unpleasant and distasteful experience to see the gaff rip in the belly or side of a good salmon or sea trout. It is a joy to bring home fish in all their pristine and unspoiled beauty, to display them and admire them.

A fish to be tailed should be brought into any convenient spot head first and be lying on its side about a rod's length from you with the rod at an angle of about 45° to the left or the right as the case might be. Always bring the fish in to one side or the other and never directly in towards your feet. If it is being brought into the left, then have the rod in your left hand with the line shortened and the left arm slightly extended to maintain a steady strain on it while you move up to the fish, bend down and catch it by the tail with right hand. Yes, it's as simple as that.

How to Hold a Sea Trout

THE accepted, correct way to grip the fish is at the thinnest point above the tail with the thumb and index finger next to the tail, that is, with the hand in a supine position. This means putting the fingers under the fish, but without doubt it makes for a very secure grip. I never do this except when tailing a fish in deep water. I have always found gripping it with the hand prone a perfectly safe method. With smaller fish of a size not easy to tail, a firm grip may be round the middle from the back, taking a secure hold with the thumb and fingertips on the fish's belly.

Once the fish is in your grip, lift it high and away from your body. If it kicks tighten your hold, but allow your arm to swing with the kicks. If you try to keep your arm rigid, then assuredly the fish will kick free from your grasp. If you are unable to lift a heavy fish with one hand, grip it securely with one hand and, gently easing the strain, lay down the rod and grip the fish with both hands at the tail. The fish will wait for you to do all this if you do so calmly. A wet but not sodden handkerchief on your hand prevents it from slipping and ensures a safe grip.

Excited grabs, jumbs and other tactics are sure to lead to trouble and, often, bitter disappointment. Never touch the line if you are tailing a fish for a fellow angler and never stand between the fish and its possible escape route. These are two common and very risky practices. I was told by a very well-known angler of a fish shooting away between his legs to its freedom when he was trying to tail it. Fortunately for him he did not have three flies on his cast or he might well have been left with one or two in his leg.

Beaching

FISH may also be landed by beaching. I do not advocate this method at all, but I know that it is carried out successfully by many people. I suspect that they use tackle slightly stronger than mine. However, mention must be made of this method because it is a proven successful method for many. A number of rivers have suitable places for beaching fish, with gently sloping shingle, sand, or even rock slabs. As soon as the fish can be made to come into the shallows the angler, with rod held up and steady pressure being maintained, should walk slowly backwards until the fish's head is out of the water and on the shore. Then he must keep up the steady pressure, waiting until the fish kicks. Continuing to maintain this steady pressure, he will find that each kick works

Beaching a fish.

the fish higher and higher up the bank. Then, when the whole body of the fish is clear of the water, he can take off the pressure, walk forwards and pick up his fish. As soon as the pressure is taken off, the fish will invariably lie quiet and still. As in tailing, all the angler's movements must be calm and steady.

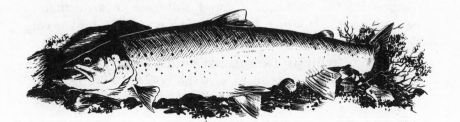

9

SOME GOOD SEA TROUT

MEMORIES flood my mind when I relax and let myself recall days and evenings on lochs and rivers in days gone by. When I was young, I was not allowed to go alone on any serious fishing trip to loch or river, but only with anybody who would go with me – non-fishers usually, because I always wanted to do the fishing myself. It was fly fishing only in those days. The tackle I used was cheap, old and maybe even unusable by present-day standards, but it taught me much.

The Oldest Sea Trout

MY first really big sea trout came in 1928. It was the finest specimen of sea trout I have ever caught, and it was a famous one too. It weighed 12½lb and was the oldest known recorded sea trout. Its capture remains as vivid as if it had happened yesterday and, although I did not know it then, I now know that that fish was the real beginning of my great luck with rod and line. The river was high but clean, and I was fishing with an 0x gut cast which was 7lb breaking strain. A Heckham and Black was the bob fly, a Grouse and Claret in the middle, and a Peter Ross on the tail. All three flies were size 8.

The run I was fishing was short and fast and the natural lie at that particular height was only two or three yards long, lying beyond shallow rough water. My father was with me and I fished from well upstream to allow me to fish the flies as slowly as I could over the lie. The tendency was for the stream to whip them away. With those first few casts and with high expectations, I rose several fish from 4 to 7 or 8lb. They were all different fish, we thought, and I missed them because I was letting the flies swing away too quickly. These fish were very black or red, whichever word one may wish to use to describe a late autumn fish, and it's likely that had they been caught they would have been put back. I brought my flies round a yard lower downstream and the extra yard meant that the flies came round a fraction slower. There was a flash in the stream and I had a fish on. I hooked it by easing the rod at the flash, which allowed the fish to turn with the fly, rather than striking. It fought well and fast and was tailed in a pool sixty yards downstream of where I first hooked it. Peter Ross was the fly it took, a favourite fly ever afterwards, justifying my faith in it many times over.

I remember that my father was more excited about that fish than I was, and we went home without fishing more. I think that he knew that the chances of getting a fish comparable to this one were nil. I also think that he was right: I have yet to see another like it. But for my luck, I'd have hooked one of the earlier red fish and never even had reason to dream about the one I did catch. Had I started fishing a few yards higher, I might well – and unluckily – have succeeded in getting my flies to linger momentarily longer over the head of the lie and, again, hooked a red fish.

That 12½lb sea trout was one of many of 9lb and over which I have recorded. There have been too many under that weight to record. It was in faster-running water than I would really have expected to fish, but later on I got several large ones in faster and heavier water than even now I would expect.

Another fish I caught a year later, 14lb and my largest to date, also came in very heavy water in the neck of a pool. It came with a splash and was on almost before I knew what had happened. I let it have the free run of the reel, but even so kept a strain on the fish. I was alone this time. The fish played well, but not wildly, and my difficulties did not arise until the end. The current was flowing fast by the boulders on my side and it wasn't until I reached a pool two hundred yards downstream that I found a lull in its flow where I was able to hold the fish in the shallows without undue strain and tail it. My small hand had difficulty in gripping it, and I got my two hands round the tail and my troubles were almost over. It too was on a Peter Ross. I had one or two other fish that day and my load was mighty heavy by the time I had carried it the two and a half miles up river to home. Years later, another good fish, 10¾lb, took me in a fast heavy water. This time it was expected, and it rose beautifully!

Premonition

BEFORE I tell of this exciting experience, I must say how I knew that I was to get a large fish at that spot. I knew that it was going to rise. I was ready for it. Knowing that a fish is going to rise happens quite frequently. It is not wishful thinking or hoping, but seems to be an indefinable attitude of mind, a sixth sense, an affinity with the fish. It's knowing that all the factors are right for the fish to take and that all that is needed is that there are fish there in that likely lie. It isn't just that I believe I am going to catch a fish – though that, too, is important for success. But it is knowing that I am to catch a fish. There are many other anglers who experience this, so it is not peculiar to me by any means. It is the same for salmon as it is for sea trout.

In recalling these captures it may seem that these wonderful catches suggest easily caught fish, but that is not so. Sometimes fish take like fury, but even then careful fishing is needed to produce the best results. Too often I have heard it said to others, as well as to me, when a good basket has been brought in that 'They must have been taking well.' A good fisherman can make the most of his chances, and the fishing need not necessarily have been easy. I have seen sea trout and salmon rising to others in a way that I've never had the good fortune to encounter, but with a poor lot to show for it at the end of the day. Why the poor result? That 'The fish were rising short' was the wrong reason given. Yet if a good angler took advantage of it his prowess would be retold with a flavour of sour grapes.

And now to return to the sea trout mentioned above. The pool was a long one with the outside of its curve on my side and the edge beside me had been sharply cut by flood water. Five feet of water flowed down fast a foot below the level on which I was standing. The curve extended for 600 yards or so, the last 200 yards being roughened by overhanging bracken and then a clump of eleven alder trees which hung over the water. The fish played well and began to tire, but there was nowhere for me to bring it in to tail it. The current swept it back that little harder than I dared attempt to overcome with my 7lb cast. Down it went slowly and almost aimlessly. I followed it to the trees. The decision to slacken my line and let the pull on the fish be exercised by the current on the line below gave me time to assess my position. This tactic usually stops a fish leaving a pool – though not always – and it must be done in time.

My situation was quite simple. I was right up against it in the form of the eleven alder trees. They were too high for me to reach over and were overhanging water which was too deep for me to wade. I climbed the first tree until I was high enough to reach out with my rod to clear the overhanging branches with my line. I went from one tree to the next, all eleven, and down to the clear bank once more. I tightened and the fish was still on. Downstream he went again, past several corners where I might have tailed him, but I was afraid to apply the little extra pressure required lest the prolonged strain over the past half-hour had weakened cast or hold. Down it went another 500 yards and out into the stream and into the loch until all my line was out. Not a turn was left on the reel. I waded out the few feet I could and stretched to the limit. There was nothing more to give at my end. Away in the distance I saw a large tail up in the air as the head was held and the fish turned over. The battle was won. I brought it almost straight in by the side of the stream and tailed it. It weighed 10¾lb.

And a Mishap

ANOTHER good sea trout which taught me a lesson came one evening while I was fishing with a friend. There were only the two of us in the boat and I had both oars well back onto the forward seat. I was able to keep the boat along the drift and fish so that both rods were in action. There was a fair wind blowing and my dropper and Black Pennell were responding beautifully under my guidance. A fish came up from nowhere, rolled on and down with the Black Pennell, and as he waved goodbye with his tail I tightened firmly but not sharply and the battle was on. My friend, an inexperienced oarsman and bulky, took the oars and with strokes which held me spellbound he guided the boat round a rocky point and onto a beach of bright shingle. As the boat approached the shingle he stood up as the bow ploughed into it. The jerk unbalanced him. He staggered and fell. There was a crack. His big backside had landed on the butt of his rod, which he had carelessly flung between the seats in his excitement to take the oars. The damage need not be described. Suffice it to say that the rod was never used again – nor, I hope, the language. He netted the fish for me, a bar of silver, 9½lb.

It is interesting to reflect that none of my sea trout worthy of recording were ever caught on the dap, although I've had a good many smaller fish on it.

The last recordable sea trout I caught was one of 10lb on Loch Hope. It was late evening and it came as I glided the boat along in dead calm water less than a minute after I had risen the largest sea trout I've ever risen – a beautiful rise but no touch, though the flies continued round in their steady curve. I was sure it would rise again but it didn't, though there had been no speeding up of the flies to make it wary, as assuredly it would have been had I made any semblance of a strike.

—10—

TACKLE

A GREAT deal has been written about the advantages and disadvantages of the vast amount of tackle available to the public. Much of what is written has the same end in view, be it the catching of salmon, sea trout, brown trout, or just a customer. Various lengths of rods are advocated by different people for the same purpose. Level lines, double-taper lines, forward-taper lines, in almost countless weights and thicknesses, are recommended. There is a multitude of reels to choose from, large and small and light and heavy.

The tackle needed is the tackle most suited to the type of fishing to be done, and that is the tackle we must decide upon. In making this decision we must consider the greatest of our fish, the sea trout, and how to catch them in darkness or daylight, dull or clear weather, in drought or flood conditions. It is wise to consider the sea trout as the shyest of fish. Whether it is or not may be a matter of opinion, but it is vital for success that it be so credited. Sometimes the fish can be a complete fool and we can hook it without difficulty, but mostly great skill is required and the more closely our fly represents the natural fly or food the greater our chance of success.

The first essential is to get the fish to rise and take our offering. The shyest will turn away from any suspicious look about the fly, so the finer the cast the better. The dapped fly, which has no nylon at all in the water, seems to be the ideal arrangement, but perhaps it is not so, as we shall consider later.

Never use a cast of 10lb BS for a 5lb fish, nor yet one of 3lb for a 5lb fish either, though both may lead to the capture of 5lb fish on occasion. To use tackle which is obviously too fine is foolish, but occasionally a calculated risk may be worth taking. In order to use the finest cast possible a light, sensitive rod and a light reel and line must be used in a receptive hand – and by a light rod I do not mean a short rod.

Balance

It is important to balance your tackle to the kind of fishing to be done, but it isn't necessary to have lots of rods, reels and lines. One rod, reel and line does well for all boat fishing for sea trout and much river fishing as well, and I find one outfit perfectly adequate for all my sea trout fishing with fly. The most improperly balanced tackle I have seen was a heavy 14-foot salmon rod with a No. 6 line and 6½lb cast.

The lightest reel is the best reel. It should hold at least 100 yards of backing and line. There are many good light reels to be had, and a good one is a sound investment, because one must never forget that a sea trout can, on occasion, be a good 100 yards away before one has really recovered from the shock of the strike!

Rods

IN considering the length and strength of the rod to be used, we must bear in mind that if we are to do any loch fishing from a boat we shall almost certainly be fishing with a cast of three flies. The cast is usually nine, ten or eleven feet in length and I think that the ideal is ten feet, giving roughly thirty inches between the flies and three feet or so of tapered nylon from the line to two feet or so from the top dropper. The taper makes for easier casting and the nylon is less visible in the water than is the line. With this 10-foot cast, a rod of more than ten feet is necessary and when a fish is being played with the rod bent a 12-foot rod is best. The danger of the join between the fly line and the loop of the leader catching in the top ring should be avoided if reasonable care and attention is taken in playing fish. Such problems are eliminated if a needle knot is used to join the leader to the fly line.

A splice of the line to the cast is often neglected and so becomes the cause of disappointment, but it does rule out the dangers associated with a knot at the top ring when playing a fish.

We must always keep to the front of our minds the shyness of the sea trout and the need to present our offering as delicately and as far off as we can control completely. We get this maximum distance with the minimum of effort with a 12-foot rod. It is extremely difficult to cast our flies with a light line on a 9-foot rod. It is easy with the heavier line, but then hurling the flies a great distance is not the primary aim of a sea trout fisher.

The short rod and the comparatively heavy line used in conjunction with it are very popular, and, in some hands, extremely effective, but with my experience of the short rod, and it's been fairly extensive, I find that it has many disadvantages – so many, in fact, that they far outweigh its advantages.

An Ideal Rod

My choice, then, is a light 12-foot rod. Farlows made the McLaren 12-foot split-cane rod for me many years ago – an excellent rod which may still be available. Now I have a 12-foot carbon rod with a 6-inch extension handle made privately by Marcus Warwick of Uppingham and called the C. C. McLaren Sea Trout Rod. It's a marvellous rod and incredibly light. I have tested it day and night for sea trout fishing as well as on many grilse and small salmon on both loch and river and it has met all my demands.

Lines

I think that the new lines are much better than the great old silk ones and they are obtainable in all weights and sizes and not a few colours. A light line is used with as fine nylon as dare be used under the conditions. This may mean a minimum of 4lb BS or a maximum of 10lb. Add to these the best flies for the area and we're almost ready to start fishing. But let's consider one or two necessary accessories before we return to the selection of line, cast, flies and the care of our tackle.

Accessories

Clothing

THE weather can be wet, windy and cold when there's fishing to be done, but seldom is it bad enough to keep us away from the water. The rain often finds an intimate and intimidating route to the skin when boat fishing, and it is a lucky angler who has found clothing which will keep him both warm and dry all day – yet this is the goal of every fisher. Gloves are not good, but fingerless mitts are a great comfort without being a nuisance when dealing with flies and playing fish.

Fly Boxes

THERE are almost as many types of fly boxes as there are flies. The small ones are best since comparatively few flies are exposed to the elements when the box is opened. With large fly boxes the flies are not always clipped in as they should be and a stumble or a puff of wind when they are opened can put many of your flies out of reach for ever more. Ensure that the clips are narrow and that they don't damage the barbs on the flies.

Boxes fitted with cork or ethaform are neat but a wet fly point will soon rust in them and I don't recommend them. What I usually do is to put wet flies into the back of the lapels of my jacket and I must confess that I usually have so many flies there that I don't really need fly boxes. A piece of cloth attached to any protective garment is handy and does rule out the need to put wet flies into a box. A rusted point can break off and a rusted eye can fray the nylon and cost the angler a good fish. Small plastic boxes are excellent for dry flies and for small double-hooked flies. The modern fishing waistcoat has everything – except the space for carrying a good fish.

Cast Carriers

THE plastic and cardboard cast carriers are excellent for storing casts in an orderly way, but you must take care not to weaken the nylon at the corners of the winder or carrier. I wind the cast round my fingers into a circle of about three inches in diameter and then put it into a cellophane envelope. This can lead to a tangle if carelessly done, but if you make it a rule to start winding at the loop of the cast or at the tail fly there is little risk of trouble. I usually start at the tail fly and finish with three turns of the loop round the coil. I start with the tail fly because I find it convenient to roll the cast from there up to the loop and then undo the knot which joins the line to the loop. I find that by doing the process in reverse the fly is free to catch up on heather or goodness knows what else, or be flicked about by the breeze, trodden on or otherwise ill-treated. When I assemble my tackle again I unwind the three turns, knot the line to the loop and then undo the coils and so avoid the dangers of the flies freely flying about.

Bags

THE fishing bag is very much a matter of personal choice as well as convenience. Again, there is a tremendous selection of bags. Choose one big enough to carry all your tackle for an outing. Choose a simple and strong design in rot-proof canvas. In fact my sporran has invariably met all my needs.

Nets

LAST but by no means least in importance is the net. Without a doubt there should be a large net in every boat. It should have a large rigid and strong hoop, but not weighty, and the handle should be three to four feet long. The ideal net for fishing is the Gye type, which has a wooden or aluminium hoop on a square shaft. The net slides down the shaft when not in use. This net has a clip which can secure it to the rim of the fishing bag or to a ring pinned to a garment, or, as I prefer, to a ring attached to a cord slung over the shoulder. It can be unclipped easily and when the handle is gripped gravity extends the net so that it's ready for use without fuss or fret. The completely collapsible net is very convenient for carrying but its greatest disadvantage is the manner in which the cross-chain or leather thong gives way, sagging under the weight of the water as the net is thrust under the fish. Instead of being straight it is curved. It is easy to misjudge its position when the net is lifted, resulting in the fish balancing on the cross-chain instead of being well over it and in the net itself. The risk of fouling flies with any net is great enough without increasing it.

The Complete Outfit

THE foregoing gives us a general picture of our needs for wet fly fishing, but now it is necessary to think in greater detail about some of the tackle. We will do so with a specific day's fishing in view – a day in a boat on a good sea trout loch.

The 12-foot rod is there, and the light-weight reel with eighty yards of backing and twenty-five yards of line is ready. The favourite flies are, let us say, Kate McLaren, Black Pennell, Grouse and Claret, and Peter Ross. We must re-member that we may get sea trout up to 10lb or more, or salmon up to 25lb, and, furthermore, the wind may be strong or gentle. In view of this it is a wise preparation to have a selection of casts made up and ready for use, whatever the conditions. In stormy weather, when there is a considerable chance of a salmon, a cast of 10lb BS nylon is advisable with a size 6 Kate McLaren or Black Pennell on the top dropper and a size 8 Peter Ross on the tail. The flies should be tied to the nylon with a two-circle turle knot and be about thirty inches apart on the cast. Droppers should be about three inches long.

The Cast

THE cast is made up of three lengths of nylon joined by blood knots. The droppers are continuations of the upper length of nylon at each knot. The top section of the cast is five feet or so in length, tapering from its butt at 10lb BS to the top dropper at 8lb. The reason for using an extension of the upper strand for the dropper is that if the lower strand were used the pull of the fish would tend to open the knot and loosen it.

Beware of making the droppers too long. They can twist themselves round the cast, which is a dreadful nuisance. It is as well to have a spare cast of each size and on this 8lb nylon a good variation would be a size 8 Black Pennell, a size 8 Grouse and Claret and a size 6 Peter Ross or Invicta. In anticipation of a nice steady breeze, which is so essential for ideal conditions, have two casts made up with 8lb nylon and the flies all size 8, in the same order as above, with the butt of the leader tapering from 10lb. If you anticipate a very light breeze, two casts of 6lb BS should be tied up with size 8 flies, as above, and two with size 10 flies, with the leader butt tapering from 8lb. These cast suggestions serve only as a guide. Seek the advice of an experienced local fisherman, as he usually knows the best flies and sizes and can advise you on the likely conditions on the loch as well as the best places to go.

Using the Tackle

THE next stage is arrival at the loch complete with tackle, appropriate clothing, food and drink. We have chosen a light 12-foot rod for a number of reasons in addition to those I have already given. It enables us to fish our dropper on the surface in a similar way to dapping. It also helps us to fish the flies slowly but not limply, which is vital in sea trout fishing, as well as having time to recast quickly over a risen

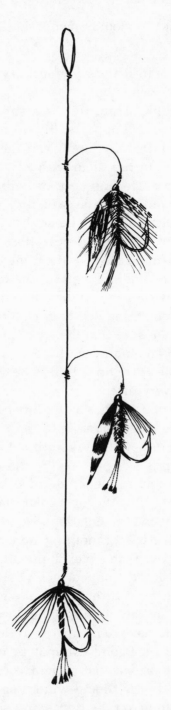

*A typical 3-fly cast (not to scale): Invicta, Grouse
and Claret, Black Pennell*

fish. It allows us to fish deeply and to derive other advantages as will be seen later.

When assembling a cane rod make sure that the ferrules fit tightly but easily. If you have any difficulty, or if you feel any stickiness in the ferrules, clean them. A good way of cleaning them is to rub them with a little bit of candle and then polish them. Do this once or twice, insert the ferrule and turn it round, and you will find that this will have cleaned it and that there will be no difficulty in dismantling the rod at night. During this operation, grip the metal part and not the cane. Twisting the cane weakens the joint between the cane and the metal at the ferrule.

When you have assembled the rod, prop it up on a bush or tree or car or something like that. Don't lay it down on the ground and make sure that the spare point is put in a safe place, either in an aluminium tube or tied to other rods. A safe place for the spare tip is under the gunwale of the boat. It fits in there very nicely.

The rod we are using has a dull finish and it doesn't glint in the sun. This is a great asset in any rod, particularly in a boat. The flash of a rod can disturb fish.

The next step is to fit the reel to the rod and the correct position of the reel is usually decided by a fixed fitting. If there is no fixed fitting the most comfortable position for the reel is found by experimentation. Secure the reel well. This is important since there is nothing more alarming or likely to be more disastrous than a reel falling off a rod when casting or playing a fish. A dropped reel may be dented with no means of repairing it at hand. It may go overboard and a hundred yards of hauling has to be done before the reel is recovered, if you have remembered to tie the backing to the drum. Even worse, a good fish may be lost.

It is a matter of personal preference whether the reel is right-hand wind or left-hand wind. I am right-handed and prefer the reel to be on the right-hand side. My reasons for preferring it so are that with the two-handed rod it is easy to change the position of the hands and the line can be wound in quicker with the right hand. It has to be done pretty smartly at times. With the left hand holding the rod the right hand is free and ready for tailing a fish. Perhaps the best reason of all is that I have always had it in that position and attempts to change have not been successful enough to convince me that a change would be to my ultimate good.

Take care to take the line off the drum in the proper place, not from under a turn of line, and out through the correct opening of the reel. Be sure that the line is threaded through all the rings. A missed ring or a turn of the line round the rod can mean a lost fish. At this stage make sure that the reel doesn't get into sand or grit, as both will soon damage its interior workings. When the rod is threaded fix on your cast, unwind it and attach the tail fly to the eyelet on the butt of the rod or to the side of the reel. When you are carrying the rod, do so with the rod tip behind.

It may seem that I have over-emphasised what not to do and what not to get, but it is really not so. These 'do nots' are important and their observation provides a firm foundation for fishing knowledge and ability without the need to learn by bitter experience.

Views on the Short Rod

THE short fly rod is in more general use for several reasons. The length of line required can be cast easily and the rod is light. It is used single-handed and so leaves the other hand free to retrieve line, and it does appear easy to use. Many good baskets and many heavy fish are killed with it and it can be used for trout, sea trout or salmon fishing. American anglers are very keen on short rods and that well-known and wonderful American fisherman, the late Joe Brooks, was a real master of the short rod. There is no denying the fact that it is perfect for certain styles of fishing. The sales talk of some fishing-tackle makers and their agents has been effective, though it has not been based on knowledge of some of the types of fishing for which it is advocated. It would not be so widely popular were it not such an excellent rod for general use, and for that reason I don't condemn it. But here we are after sea trout, sea trout only, and with the short rod a comparatively heavy line is required, even for boat fishing, and I am too aware of the advantages of the light line to forgo them.

Boats

ALWAYS make sure that a boat is safe before you use it. Some points one should know and some one must know. The floorboards should be correctly positioned. Their function is an important one and not merely ornamental. They protect the ribs and planks which are between you and the deeps below. Oars can slip through rowlocks and be lost. Many boats are fitted with pin oars and they are excellent for fishing, though I must confess that I don't like them when rowing. The round oars with rowlocks can be tied with cord to the gunwale, so the real danger of accidental loss is removed.* If an oar is used to push the boat out from the shore, use the handle and not the blade. Blades are very easily broken and a broken oar is useless.

Most fishing boats are of such a size that it is not wise to stand up in them, particularly if there is a wave about. Care is essential. It may be that I am particularly cautious, but I don't think my caution is misplaced. It is probably because I cannot swim and it would be good were all boat-users to behave as though they couldn't swim either. When a boat is beached, don't leave it rocking on the shore. Pull it well up and secure it firmly. With heavy rain the loch might rise many feet during the night and you may want to use the boat next day.

* The same applies to the outboard motors – T.G.L.

—11—

CASTING

It was in 1676 that Charles Cotton wrote:

> The length of your line, to a Man that knows how
> to handle his Rod, and to cast it, is no manner of
> encumbrance . . . and the length of line is a mighty
> advantage to the fishing at a distance; and to fish
> *fine, and far off* is the first and principal Rule for
> Trout Angling.

He could well have included sea trout angling in this advice.

Long Casting

In my young days, more often than not, my success with the rod and line depended upon my ability to cast a long line, especially to enable me to reach lies which others hadn't. In those early days I learned how great and vital was the difference between casting a fly long distances and fishing a fly at a long distance. There are many lies in most rivers which can be reached, but not fished, by most anglers. They might be reached by the angler casting his maximum distance and usually with the maximum effort, though great effort is quite unnecessary to gain maximum distance – such casts usually land smack on top of the lie, and that is not the way to treat the sea trout. A stance other than that nearest to the lie may be needed in order to make the flies fish properly over it without landing with a splash over the fish. If it is made upstream of the lie, the cast may straighten out and the flies be fishing well before being brought round to the lie. In this way a long cast poorly executed may still be fished properly.

I usually fish as short a line as the average angler because I learned a long time ago that casting a long line when a short one was needed was just as unproductive as casting a short one when a long one was necessary. This applies to most types of fishing, whether for trout feeding close inshore, sea trout and salmon lying close to the near bank, or the fish by the far bank. Experience and knowledge are needed to know where to find your fish. It is the person who can both reach and fish the lie at the far bank as well as the one at the near bank who has the greatest success.

I know many good anglers who are content with their style and who won't make any effort to improve their casting techniques. They discount the advantages of good casting by arguing that they catch as many fish as the next man. Sometimes they do. I will concede that point, because at least 60 per cent of the anglers I meet are good casters, or can put out a long enough line to enable them to kill fish tolerably well. Nowadays the standard of casting is higher – even though the tackle used to achieve distance cannot always be called fine.

Rods and Lines

THE tackle I used from the beginning generally consisted of a 12-foot rod and a light level line. Many days spent using the short rod with lines of various weights, as well as the exercise of much patience and concentration, has brought me to my deep-seated preference for the long rod. I was fortunate in having ample opportunity of using a great variety of makes and sizes of both rods and lines, and on reflection, I would say that the vast majority of rods are rated for lines too heavy to obtain the maximum distance. I think they are rated thus to flatter poor casters rather than to obtain the best performance.

The Teaching of Casting

CORRECT casting must be taught and in the past it hasn't always been possible to get good tuition from a good caster. By a good caster I don't mean a good average caster but a good teacher who knew what he was teaching. There are now some excellent instructors throughout the country, but, alas, also some poor ones. Casting a good line is not as difficult as many would have us believe – there are no great hidden mysteries in casting well.

The effort needed to become efficient in casting is quite considerable, but it is well worthwhile. Remember that good casting can make fishing easy, whereas tackle designed to make casting easy may make the fishing of lies very difficult. Using a heavy line along with a very fine cast is, for instance, bad for fishing, even if good for distance casting.

Tournament Casting

I FIRST heard of tournament casting in the 1950s. I took an interest in it and have found out all I want to know about it. Pressure of work forced me to give it up, but it was good fun, enlightening and satisfying to a degree. With luck I shall dabble in it again, but only dabble. Much of it is for men of tougher fibre than one of 5 feet 8 inches and ten stone, with an army pension to boot.

Tournament casting and competitions are decried by the vast majority of anglers and, I must admit, these competitions are pretty weary at times. So much of the tackle used is completely useless for fishing. Much of it, though not all, cannot be defended, even on the grounds of being on a test run. That principle may be of value to the manufacturers of racing cars, but the rhythm, timing and smoothness of action of the expert caster are essential to get the maximum distance and accuracy from any tackle. Strength does not compensate for all casting faults, though it does for quite a few, and, of course, it is of great advantage when used in a properly controlled way.

I was a long caster by nature and my involvement in tournament casting followed a meeting with and much help from the late Tommy Edwards. I put as much thought and time into practice as I could and was rewarded in competitions. My participation in tournament casting made a tremendous difference to my fishing. Distance, accuracy and control of both the fly and the bait all improved vastly. At any time when fishing I can derive a great deal of pleasure out of the execution of a particular cast.

Casting technique can be improved very quickly, but, sadly, fishing ability grows only with experience. Freedom from casting worries allows for greater concentration and the better presentation of fly and bait. The trees and breeze don't cause insurmountable problems to the able caster, but they may prove serious to the poor caster who may not be able to continue fishing under the same conditions. There is no need to cast a long line all the time – far from it – but to be able to do so when needed will certainly add to the weight of fish carried home.

Competitions

MORE and more interest is being taken in casting competitions every year and more demonstrations are being given by experts. This is good, because better casting leads to better fishing, or should. Great distances need not be cast and the angler need not fear being belittled if his performance doesn't measure up to that of the expert.

I remember one small competition when a well-known angler in the area tried to compete and gave it up in disgust. This isn't an unusual reaction, for what seems a long cast in fishing often is not when measured from the casting point. This illusion creates opposition to competitions in some angling circles. It is a great pity, because it is precisely through these casting competitions that casting can be improved and be shown to improve in an enjoyable way. The technique for correct casting is the same for everyone who uses a rod and line, whether for the capture of fish or the making of casting records.

Casting competitions with specialised tackle no longer seem to be as popular as they once were, but they are still important enough from the point of tackle development. I hear and see little about them now which seems to indicate that there is no longer the interest there once was. However, casting competitions using ordinary fishing tackle (skish) are held throughout the country and they continue to be good fun as well as of great benefit to the thoughtful angler.

Reading

THERE are several good books on casting, excellently illustrated. *The Angler's Cast* by Tommy Edwards and Eric

Horsfall Turner, *Casting* by Terry Thomas and *A Fly Fisher's Life* by Charles Ritz are all good, as of course, are the fishing books of Hugh Falkus, Bill Currie, Arthur Oglesby and Conrad Voss Bark.

Technique

I SHALL refer to technique only briefly. I have found that great benefit is derived by pupils from practising with a line too light for the rod. The correct action is essential with this equipment and the distraction of achieving distance is not great. It is casting not in practice but in actual fishing that taught me the correct rhythm. Advice varies considerably, but if it achieves good casting it cannot be criticised.

The line must be kept parallel with the ground, or nearly so, during the back cast and while the line is unrolling. This means that the degree beyond the vertical in which the power must be continued varies with the strength of the wind blowing towards you from behind. A good back cast is essential if a good fore cast is to be made. I frequently get pupils to cast into the wind if it is the back cast which is giving them trouble. Creating the habit of watching the back cast is a great benefit to fishing. Snags behind can be avoided, small openings in the branches of trees can be utilised. The power in the back cast and in the forward cast must be applied at a critical moment, especially with the light line. There is not the same in-built assistance from this line as there is from the heavy line, so the pupil has to work at producing it.

Some Common Faults

THERE are a few faults common to many anglers and it is often a very simple fault that prevents them from becoming first-class casters and will continue to do so until it is detected and corrected.

Stance

STANCE is unimportant to the person who fishes a lot. It is not always easy to obtain a good stance, nor have we the time to seek one before making each cast. Nevertheless, it is important for the extra-long cast as well as acting as a remedy for many faults. One particular trouble arises from bringing the rod round to the side in a sweep, so that the line is travelling almost horizontally. This is aggravated if a right-hand caster has his left foot forward (or a left-handed his right foot). It allows the body to turn easily with the arm. A right-handed caster can solve it to a considerable degree by putting his right foot forward and thus fixing the pelvis and reducing the range of body rotation. If the angler practises with a wall fairly close on his right-hand side he is forced to keep the rod nearer to the vertical position.

Incorrect stance is a fault of some really excellent anglers I know. They could cast a tremendous length of line if they managed to overcome this problem and would do so with much less effort too. The power applied must not only impel the line backwards and forwards but also change its sweeping direction.

Lifting Too Much Line

DIFFICULTIES arise from attempting to lift too much line out of the water at the beginning of the back cast and not applying the power until too late in the back cast. When ther is too much line out it is better to make a switch or roll cast first.

Holding Too Tightly

ANOTHER beginner's fault is that of holding the rod too tightly. In addition both the wrist and the body are too rigid, so that both rod and arm are wielded as though they were a stick. Hold the rod firmly but allow it to give a little with the wrist, with a slight easing of the joint when the power has been applied. To hold a rod too fiercely is not only very tiring but also blister-inducing.

A good fly caster is a good bait caster, naturally. The reverse is not the case.

Shooting Line

THE secret of shooting line lies in releasing the line to be shot immediately after the application of the power in the forward cast has been completed. With the light line I use I find that often so much line is required that to give the right weight outside the point of the rod to make the cast some must be released in the back cast if extra forward casting is to be avoided.

Changing Direction

ANOTHER difficulty many meet is that of changing the direction of the cast. The rod may be pointing downstream and the next cast is going to be very nearly across the stream. If the cast is made while the rod is pointing downstream at the start of the cast and the direction is changed in the air, the angler will experience considerable difficulty in completing this movement satisfactorily. A false cast may be made to bring it half-way to the new direction and then the next cast may be correct. It would be better to bring the rod point round to the direction in which the next cast is to be made before the line is lifted from the water. Make the cast from there and all will be well.

A Myth

I HAVE always been lucky in fishing and often caught fish of both size and quality under such adverse conditions as to have the reputation as a good angler thrust upon me in various parts of Britain as well as abroad. I could talk to knowledgeable anglers about fishing and, at times, I felt encouraged to venture to propound my own ideas about it. Since I took an interest in tournament casting and became associated with it, I have had to listen to a lot of talk about how tournament casters can cast but not fish, as well as a lot of other rubbish about the tackle used at these tournaments.

I prefer my old status of ordinary angler, but I cannot do any other than defend the tournament caster.

Casting is part of fishing and top-class tournament casters can cast, let there be no doubt about that. I do not say that all tournament casters can fish. Some I have seen have not had the opportunity to fish widely and gain varied experience by fishing months on end each year. Some are run-of-the-mill fishermen. The majority are very fine anglers.

When you get the chance, go and watch the expert. Examine his tackle and technique and you will see that there is no trickery in it. You will enjoy the sight of properly executed casting. You will learn a lot. You will fish a lot better after it, too. When casting, generally picture the land behind and the water in front as being a few feet higher than they really are. This is a great help.

─────12─────

Unwritten Laws

A FEW words which apply to many aspects of fishing may be helpful. Courtesy costs nothing, but often it is lacking in angling as in everything else because of ignorance of the etiquette or ignorance of the unwritten rules of fishing rather than through lack of sportsmanship.

Angling Queues

WHEN fishing a river which is so crowded with anglers that everyone adopts a stance nearly shoulder to shoulder few attempt to move and most, if not all, wade. Apparently it is too much to see a smoothly moving queue system, yet, undesirable as it may be, with so many anglers and so little fishing in some areas it could be possible. Of course, it is not always needed nor is it always advisable. In some estuaries the fish do the moving.

There are a number of quieter parts of the country where one can expect to find fishing which is shared with only a comparatively small number of other anglers and there are some dos and don'ts worth remembering which make for happy relations with everyone.

Speed of Fishing

IF someone is fishing a pool, whether on your own bank or on the opposite one, let him fish down a considerable distance before starting to fish at the neck of the pool. Or, better still, let him finish fishing the pool completely before starting. Of course, if the river is a wide one what is going on on the bank opposite may not concern you in any way. This prevents the other angler from feeling rushed and also allows the pool to be rested a little before being fished again.

When you fish down the pool do so reasonably quickly at, say, two casts every three steps. If you rise a fish, the fish is yours to rest for a minute or two before trying again. Don't spend too long on it. A fellow angler will gladly leave you time to catch it and, indeed, if there is plenty of other fishing he will probably leave you to it. This is a good principle in any case, rise or no rise.

Claiming a Pool

You may wish to stay at a pool for a long time. By all means do so, but let others fish through if they appear on the scene and don't try to claim the pool or stream for your own exclusive use. The same applies to fishing a loch from the bank. Move on at a reasonable pace or let others fish through if they wish. Overcrowding can take place during night fishing, too, and not all refrain from rushing to where a fish is seen or heard, irrespective of how much other anglers may be considering each other.

Bank Behaviour

WHETHER returning to the neck of the pool or walking to another stretch of the river, keep as far back from the side as you can. This is particularly important if the bank is much above water level or of the type to be a good conductor of vibration – in other words, anything other than rock or shingle. Don't stand or walk silhouetted against the sky and keep your rod low, with its tip to the rear. Even the shadow of a rod falling across a stream can disturb sea trout. Some other angler may be hiding behind the proverbial blade of grass, using all his skill and experience in trying to catch a particular fish. Your shadow, silhouette or vibration could defeat him. It could also disturb fish which you yourself may be fishing for later.

Conversation

THE angling fraternity are really a friendly lot, but one of the great joys in fishing is the complete escape it can give from everyday work, worries and windbags. All cares are forgotten. A word of greeting is fine, but if the other fellow wants your company as well as hearing your theories, he will ask for them. Talk is not for the riverside, unless invited. Keep it for other times when memories and discussions have to take the place of fishing. The winters are long! Great earnestness and concentration may be needed for successful fishing at times, so leave the angler in peace to apply it. Let his contest be with the fish only.

When watching a fish being played, keep well away and don't cause any distraction. Any advice sought will be called for. When giving assistance do as asked – even if you think you know a better way of doing whatever it may be. Most anglers know what they want done, be it right or wrong. It is better that they themselves are responsible for the capture or loss of the fish.

Loch Manners

ON a loch don't take a boat by oar or engine across the drift in front of another boat fishing that drift, or at any other time if it can be avoided. The less the sea trout are subjected to such disturbance the better the fishing for all. Normally a boat's drift is from one main point of a bay to the other main point. It is in order to start a drift at the next point down-wind, provided that the other boat is not too close. An exception to this is when there are points in a recognised and usually named drift. Better to keep away altogether and so avoid having as well as giving that feeling of crowding.

When going upwind or downwind keep well away from any drifting boat so that the wash from your bow doesn't reach the water being fished. Sea trout which have been up for a few days can be so easily disturbed that the wash from the bows of a passing boat can make all the difference between a fish taking the fly and rising short. Don't take your boat upwind on the inside of a short drift. The wash carries out a long way and fish may be lying close to the shore. These fish will be disturbed and, in darting out to the deeper water, disturb other fish. This kind of disturbance of possible taking fish by frightened fish is most evident in a river. Stealth, once so important in the days of plenty, is even more important for success in these leaner times.

Sometimes you may be tempted to keep the bow of the boat into the wind and let it slip back slowly as the water is being fished. This is usual on some lochs where there is only one boat on the beat, or where other boats do likewise. Without doubt it is the best way of holding a boat for one-rod fishing, but it must be avoided if another boat wishes to drift the stretch. It is just like trying to claim a pool on a river.

'Poaching' in a Boat

WHEN you share a boat don't 'poach' on the other fellow's water. You have as much water to fish as he and, if the boat tends to run in your direction, leave some unfished water for your friend following you at the other end of the boat. Fishing a short line will do this.

Any fish which has been foul-hooked should be returned to the water.

Bait Fishing

BAIT fishing and spinning do spoil the water for the fly fisher, unless the water is useless for the fly or the sea trout are running. Don't fish with bait or spinner in good fly water except by agreement with the other anglers. I am not advocating a ban on the bait fisherman – far from it. There are forms of bait fishing and spinning which call for the highest degree of skill, equalling that of any other form of fishing – though the purist will not admit this.

What I am advocating is, as far as possible, the prevention of a clash of interest by the waterside. It is a comfort to know that the fly is very much more deadly for sea trout on a loch than either bait or spinner, more deadly than a spinner anywhere, and more deadly than the worm in a river, except in white water and when the fish are running, or, of course, when the water is out of order for fly, that is when coloured by rising flood water and dirty.

I have heard it said that the purpose of fishing is to catch fish. That may be so, but it is not all of fishing. Legal bait fishing and spinning do not always produce the fish, but they open the door to other methods which do so, and illegally. The fishing we are considering is a sport.

The Law

THE legal position in respect of brown trout fishing in Scotland is simple. It is not illegal to fish for brown trout except in tarns and where a protection order is in force, or perhaps where an area has been designated an SSSI (Site of Special Scientific Interest). But it does infringe the owner's rights, so do please get permission. It is illegal to fish anywhere for sea trout without permission, but it is an unwritten law that the trout angler should always give way to the salmon and sea trout fisher. I do not make this point from any wish to distinguish between classes of fishermen, but purely as an aid to better fishing for all. Here we are considering sea trout fishing. The brown trout fisherman will spoil the fishing for the sea trout man but the reverse is not the case. Brown trout soon forget the disturbance, but not so the sea trout. It may not always be practicable to apply all this, but it is worth bearing in mind.

When renting a fishing which may seem to be expensive, enjoy it without worrying about trying to catch enough to pay the rent and you won't have the temptation to fetch fish which will not come of their own free will, and you won't, in the process, forget that fishing is a sport. I know of fishings which are not worth half the rent asked and collected so far as the return in fish is concerned but are in such wonderful surroundings that their value to a true sportsman and lover of nature can never be assessed. In seeking permits for fishing, remember that a great many who have control over it may only get limited time for fishing themselves and, quite naturally, they wish to make the most of it.

Local Rules and Regulations

WHEREVER you fish, find out all the local rules and regulations. Be anti-litter-minded and, with such vast areas of new plantations, be ever conscious of inadvertently causing a fire.

Some extra rules might be useful – for example, limiting the number of rods to a specific area at certain times; having a beat system for boats; limiting the use of outboard engines; giving experienced fishery managers more authority over the behaviour of permit-holders.

The laws of Scotland are deeply rooted in tradition and if we can all observe them we may help towards the preservation and improvement of the fishings, leading to more fishing becoming available and, ultimately, to the greater enjoyment of all our fishing expeditions.

Finally, remember:

> A' days are guid for the fishing,
> but a' days are no guid for catching' fush.

— APPENDIX 1: THE KATE MCLAREN —

The Kate McLaren was first tied by William Robertson of Glasgow, and named after John McLaren's wife, Kate (the author's mother).

Tail: Golden pheasant crest
Body: Black ribbed flat silver
Hackles: Black tied down body and at the head a natural red hen, one tied over the black (must be hen so as to work properly in the water)

—Appendix 2: Flyfishers' Knots—

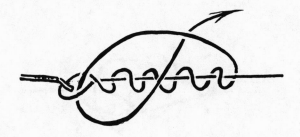

a)   Tucked half blood knot

b) Tucked sheet bend knot

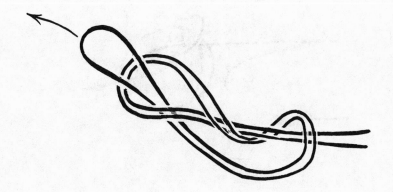

c) **Blood Blight knot**

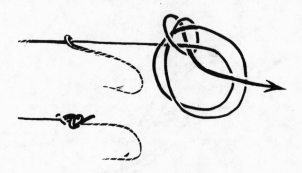

d) Two circle turle knot

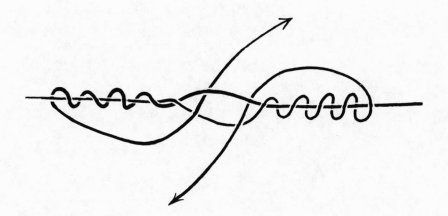

e) **Double four fold blood knot**